WARTIME I

(The sequel to *Growing*

Kathleen Healy

ARTHUR H. STOCKWELL LTD.
Elms Court · Ilfracombe · Devon
Established 1898

British Library Cataloguing-in-Publication Data.
A catalogue record for this book is available
from the British Library.

By the same author:
Growing up in a Welsh Valley

ISBN 0 7223 3313-7
Printed in Great Britain by
Arthur H. Stockwell Ltd.
Elms Court   Ilfracombe
Devon

CONTENTS

Illustrations set between pages 32 - 33

Chapter One

Leaving the Valley for War Work

My sister Mary, met me at Stroud (Gloucester) Station around 3 p.m., as my train pulled in. Together we climbed the wide wooden steps and crossed the bridge to the station exit.

In front of us, were two very large buildings. On the left-hand side, a four-storey known as "Holloway Institute" and on the right, "The Imperial Hotel". These two buildings together with "The Subscription Rooms" were "taken over" by the Air Ministry for the duration of the war and housed their permanent staff, both male and female, who originally worked at Head Office, Adastral House, Kingsway in London. Other staff were temporary, having applied for vacancies through Air Ministry advertisements.

We entered Holloway Institute and walked up the stairs to the third floor, where the typing pool was situated, and there, Mary introduced me to Miss Clements, who was the supervisor in charge. She then left me, until 6 p.m., when the office closed and we both walked home; me to my new billet.

Miss Clements was a lady, possibly in her forties, auburn haired, wearing thick lenses. She smiled at me as she shook my hand, then proceeded to introduce me to the other staff. Miss Laughey (pronounced Laffy) who was "second in command", both ladies being permanent civil servants, was a tall slim girl with an Irish brogue; she too wore spectacles; she was attractive and helpful at all times, and appeared to be around thirty years of age. Miss Clements then proceeded to introduce the other girls, one by one, then showed me where I would be sitting. My desk, being the furthest from the long window, shed very little light onto my typewriter, which looked as if it was due for retirement any day. It was a very old long carriage Olympia.

"Tea" break soon followed, and one of the girls made the tea in a room on the second floor. She carried the mugs down the stairs, one on each finger; of course they sat shakily on a tray, when she returned. The stairs were extremely wide, although narrow in depth, they were not "well lit", and besides each step being reinforced with metal; it could be dangerous.

As she handed me my mug, we both realised we had met before. She had been one of the pupils from Ystradgynlais (Wales) who took the "shorthand, typing and book-keeping course" at Glanffrwd School in Pontardawe. She had been a 'strong-willed' girl, who was a disturbance to the whole class and Mr George in particular. I had kept my distance at that time but, here I was now; in a close proximity and I knew I would need to stand up to her, and I was quite prepared to do so.

At 6 p.m. we covered our typewriters, and left the office. Mary was waiting outside to walk me to my new home in nearby Cainscross, a small village twenty minutes from the office.

We arrived at the four terraced cottages; Mary lived at no. 1, with a young couple in their early thirties. She then introduced me to Mrs Powell, at no. 3, who was to be my landlady for the best part of my stay in Stroud. She showed me my room, which was at the top of the house at the rear, under the eaves. It was very pretty, it had all the necessary facilities and a beautiful view from the small window, down to the garden, and beyond to the station halt. Originally, the four cottages had been a school. There was access to the lower floor at the rear on either side of the block of four. This was the busiest part of the house, as the cobbled stone yard held a double wash house (back to back) for nos. 1 and 2, and the same for us — nos. 3 and 4. This was where the toilet facilities were, detached from the houses themselves. The living room on this level was quite large and sunny.

The gardens were divided into four very long strips, narrow paths separated one from the other and reached down to the canal, where two swans glided along gracefully on the water, and where the neighbours passed the time of day on Sunday mornings; if not at church. The other side of the canal, there was a station halt to Gloucester, a smaller shuttle train stopped there for passengers.

Both Mr and Mrs Powell were about similar ages. "Lizzie", as her husband addressed her, was extremely tall, and full of fun! She also wore spectacles and had to remove them from 'time to time' to wipe off the tears she shed from laughing! Arthur, or "Arth", was a small bespectacled man, and rolled his own cigarettes. He smoked constantly although he suffered from ulcers, and always sat in the same armchair near the fireplace, when not working half days with his two nephews; who had a butcher's shop in Stroud near the top of the lanes.

The fact that he worked there, would normally be a boon — but I was never to enjoy special meals and never saw sausages, steak or other mouthwatering food. Most of my meals were salads with a little cheese, or a slice of corned beef. Evening dinners, boiled rice with treacle on top; although Mary had no problem with regard to her meals, one could smell the cooked breakfasts most mornings, and also being two years older than me, earned ten shillings extra; so that was pocket money.

The first morning I awoke at no. 3, I realised I was now away from home, and burst into tears, although I was in nice surroundings, I had a pretty room and a large comfortable bed, but I was with strangers. I felt like catching the next train home. I was sure I would not get used to it, but the fact I could always leave my job; cheered me on!

I saw very little of Mary, she worked in the opposite direction to our billet, at the Meteorological Office in Stonehouse. I never saw her office.

Chapter Two

The Air Ministry in Stroud

However, at 8.30 a.m., I was leaving for my walk to work in Stroud. The journey along the main road, to the Air Ministry was pleasant all the way; plenty of trees and shrubs were in bloom along the sides of the road.

This was my first day, I arrived at my office, and I was about to sit down at my desk, where now, it seemed ever darker than the day before; so — I decided there and then to tell Miss Clements that there was insufficient light for me to work in comfort; could she not, perhaps, rearrange the seating? I waited for her comments, she looked puzzled, but my eye caught Miss Laughey and she 'winked' at me, so I presumed Miss Clements would find a way of solving my problem, and this she did.

During the lunch break, she had found a strong man to move the desks around, and I was now sitting next to a very nice girl, named Barbara. Barbara sat side on to the window and I was next to her. She was a local girl and we got on fine. Her parents owned the Railway Hotel, on the main road, opposite the entrance to our short cul-de-sac, next to the station. That still left the Welsh girl with her back to the window, sitting close to Miss Clements. So all seemed happy.

My work was placed on my desk each morning. I was dealing with casualties. RAF, officers, who were either "missing", "missing presumed killed", or "killed". We worked on one stack of a particular heading at a time; together with the names to be typed in by us. I had to type in the rank, name and number, then cross him off the list. It seemed so callous, but the girls did not think so, they had possibly gone through the same emotion as I was going through at the moment; and so each day was a repeat of the previous day, although the stack never seemed to grow smaller; in fact, more were added to what was taken away — so the stack remained the same.

By the end of my first week — payday arrived. We each took our turn in collecting and signing for our wage packet. Mine was 27/6 (£1.38) per week; less:- landlady's allowance £1.1s. (£1.06) which she drew on an

8

allowance book. The balance I signed for — 6s. 6d., or 33p was the princely sum I could call my own each week. There were no luxuries for me for at least a year. We were known as "The Guinea Pigs" and each year, splashed in bold print across the headlines of newspapers read:– *"Guinea Pigs to get 5 Shillings Increase Per Week"*.

I was two months short of my eighteenth birthday when I joined the Air Ministry, early April 1940. And when I left the service in 1943, I was receiving £2.5.0. (£2.25p), less £1.1s. deducted for my landlady. From the adverts for shorthand secretaries, they were now recruiting for clerical, with no experience necessary. I met several girls I knew from Trebanos and from Ponty. One named Phyllis Williams had served in "Jenkins Cash Stores" in Herbert Street, Pontardawe for several years; she was fortunate she had a good billet with plenty of food, plus being three or four years older than myself — so monetarily was also better off than myself; yet Grammar School education and experienced shorthand typist earned you nothing extra.

I was beginning to settle in with Mr and Mrs Powell. She called me Kathleen; Mr Powell always addressed me as 'lass'. Most evenings they played cards or dominoes, and I joined in with them. They also had a dartboard which lived on the door, leading up the stairs to the sitting room and their bedroom. An even steeper, although shorter staircase then led to my bedroom and the 'spare room' in the attic. The reason the dartboard had 'pride of place' on the door, was Mr Powell's "love of darts", and any caller seeing it — Mr Powell would then say "Beat you double top", and I never knew anyone not to respond! I did try to throw the darts but they went in all directions — I did not know why, at that time in my life, but later on, an X-ray showed I had two fractured shoulders from my accident with the milk float. It was always painful to reach anything higher than normal, or to hold up a newspaper to read.

Mrs Powell, introduced the young lady in no. 2 to me, her name was Florence, and she had the dearest little baby boy; he would be six months I would say and his name was Michael. His daddy worked on transport and should it be a Saturday night — she would ask me to sleep the night, as she was scared to be alone, and I would always reply, "Yes, but only if I can cuddle Michael in bed, on Sunday mornings." Of course, we both cuddled him and he loved it.

The occupants of no. 4, were a lady in her sixties, and her elder son Norman, who was thickset and smartly turned out. He was the manager of the gentlemen's department in the Co-operative Stores just along the road. He never stopped to chat but always acknowledged you with a 'good morning'. I often heard him whistling in the 'wash house'.

Besides Norman, there were two more sons, both serving in 'The Air Force'. The middle son, named Ken, was reserved and shy but usually

9

polite. The younger son was Jack. "Jack the Lad." We always knew when he was "home on leave"! He would be the "sole survivor" from a lorry full of men coming home on leave, when the lorry had a "head-on collision" with a bus and everyone on the bus was killed too! He was "sole survivor" on most manoeuvres he went on, and he would seek out various neighbours to enlighten them of his sheer luck. Poor Jack, back at camp, he could have been a "loner".

Mrs Ersell's home, no. 4, was like a "den" — she was a tailoress by trade, and always busy. Taking up her offer of a 'cup of tea' one weekend, I stepped inside and saw lengths of material with paper patterns pinned to them, all around the room; even the curtains were made use of and the tablecloth! It was dark and depressing.

Mrs Powell's home was very 'bright and tidy'; the door always ajar, with an added net curtain to prevent any flies coming in. The floor, of course, was stone and kept the room cool.

I had been billeted some weeks now with Mr and Mrs Powell and I was about to leave for the office one morning, when the noisy arrival of heavy footsteps on the cobbled stones was heard outside; before a tall tired soldier appeared in the doorway — both hugged each other tightly, the tears fell down her cheeks; "Oh son, son, you're home and safe" she said. They both had tears in their eyes by then. I quietly left for work.

It was the first week of "The evacuation of 335,490 men from Dunkirk", and she had her George home safely.

I arrived home from the office that evening and was introduced to a very smart nice looking soldier. He was about six foot four inches tall, his hair was thick and dark, he had a neat moustache, a nice smile and "laughing eyes". The excitement in the house was electric. George was a lieutenant based not far away with the Wiltshire Regiment, attached to the Monmouth Regiment. Originally a Territorial with the Wiltshires. He was happy to spend his short 'leaves', twenty-four hours or forty-eight hours in no. 3, and early mornings his rendering of "Old Man River" was quite refreshing, as he polished his boots in the 'wash house' doorway. If his leave pass happened to be any weekend then "auntie" as George called Mrs Powell, would pass on the message from "vicar at church" — Would he kindly sing "solo" in church, and at the end of the service, lead the "choir with another hymn"?

He was always "happy to oblige" and looking straight ahead, would lead the lads to the vestry as the service ended. Then he would join us outside and we ambled the ten minutes home. Here was a very attractive man, possibly twenty-three years of age, of smart appearance; we liked each other immediately.

During the evenings, the four of us chatted together and the time flew by. When the clock struck 10 p.m., both Mr and Mrs Powell would decide to leave "us younger ones" and 'turn in' for the night. George regularly found his pipe, and leaning against the mantelpiece, filled it, but never lit it. He would search my face with a 'teasing smile', as by now, I was standing near him; yet neither of us spoke a word! I promised myself I would start a conversation if he did not, on his next leave. Before being called up with the Territorials, George worked with Thomas Stevens & Sons, a firm of underwriters in London, and was a popular member of the staff.

Regularly, after Mr and Mrs Powell had retired for the night, once 11 p.m. arrived, I would say "Time for the little wooden hill" and he would reply "Race you!" and run up the first flight which was long and curved. Once I attempted the second shorter, although steeper flight, he would hold out his hand and give me a "pull-up". Now we were facing each other with only a yard between his door and mine. Again, there would be complete silence, a twinkle in his eyes, yes, I longed to reach up and kiss him good night, but never did — we would say 'sleep tight' and I would turn and enter my bedroom, as he did on the left, and entered his room.

Once when he had left and returned to his unit, I did wonder what his room would be like? I opened the door — there among lots of empty cardboard boxes and other odds and ends, stood this very narrow single bed, a couple of blankets and a pillow. I did not like myself for intruding.

Each short 'leave pass', he would be home, and we all looked forward to his visits. Returning early morning to Wiltshire, Mrs Powell would get all giggly and say to me, "Come Kathleen, we can see George on the station platform, from your bedroom window." And there he was waiting for the "shuttle train", and she waving and tearful yet laughing as well, but there was no response from George; he was an officer and a soldier, and they don't go waving back! With his luggage in one hand and his baton in the other, how could he?

Mrs Powell had a daughter named Dorothy, she was a few years older than George; she was married and living in Cheltenham. By the time of George's next leave, Dorothy had just come out of the maternity hospital with a baby girl. Her first child. Mrs Powell told me Dorothy and George were always wrestling and chasing each other, she should have been a boy!

At Mrs Powell's suggestion, George asked me if I would like to go to Cheltenham with him on the bus to Dorothy's home and see the baby. I, of course, said yes, and we sat upstairs on the bus all the way, and closely, yes.

Arriving at Dorothy's home, George rang the bell. Dorothy opened the

11

door, saw him, gave him a 'wallop', then ran through the garden — he chased after her and they wrestled for a while, then calmed down and came indoors! She soon had tea on the table and suggested to him — he should take me into Cheltenham and show me the beautiful park, along the main road. By the time we would return, she would have a meal waiting for us. But not all was that simple, as we walked along slowly, so many army cadets saluted George, he changed sides with me, and he was now on the side nearest the traffic.

We had not gone far, when an army jeep screeched to a halt beside us, three tough-looking soldiers in heavy woollen sweaters and camouflage trousers, grabbed George; not a word was spoken; but they pushed him into the rear of the jeep and pulled the flap down, then roared away!

I did not know Cheltenham at all, so I decided I should stay where I was. No doubt there was some mistake, and he would return in the jeep to that particular spot. After half an hour, I was beginning to worry, then I saw the jeep come tearing along, and this time, George stepped out of the passenger's seat, smiles all round and an apology to me. He had been arrested in mistake for an officer who was on the "wanted list", and he answered the description "perfectly". They would not check his papers until he was interrogated by a higher authority and the War Office headquarters was at Cheltenham for the duration of the war.

We moved on to spend an hour in the park, then back to Dorothy's to admire the baby. Dorothy started another chase, when she said she reckoned he was the "wanted officer" and they were correct the first time! They should have handcuffed him!!

When George returned to base, Mrs Powell told me that at the age of ten years, she had brought George and two other boys to live with them. She longingly wanted a larger family; and she applied to Dr Barnados. George was a dear son to them and a pal to Dorothy. The two were good friends. The other two boys did not turn out as she had hoped — they were always in trouble and the trouble would escalate if they stayed, so they left.

The wash house in the yard, was used for most work. Besides housing a private separate flush toilet, there was a large copper, a butler sink and tap, plus a long galvanised bath, which hung on a large hook on the wall; and Friday nights were to be mine for bathing and washing my hair, without interruption. It was surprising how long it took to heat the water.

I saw little of my sister Mary, I don't know how she spent her time; we were living only a few yards apart.

I had been at the Air Ministry about two weeks, when I decided to walk into Stroud on the Saturday afternoon, and look around the different streets.

Stroud was a busy bustling town, narrow pavement streets ran parallel up towards the Subscription Rooms, where outside was a four-sided monument with a large clock on each face. The building was used for concerts, including band concerts. Now the Air Ministry housed their clerical staff there.

Standing talking to a smartly dressed fair-haired man was Mary; (possibly mid-thirties). As I walked towards them, he said to Mary "Who is this?"

She looked at me and in no uncertain terms, she told me to "Clear off" and to the man she said "She happens to be my sister and unfortunately she lives in Cainscross near me!"

I wrote home fairly regularly and so did Mary. All her letters told Mam that if I were to be murdered one night, it would not be her fault, as I was out, all hours of the nights with other girls who stayed out late, and were common girls. I was doing no such thing, I was indoors evenings, having no money to go anywhere, it also being pitch-dark with the blackout. Possibly, on reflection, by keeping me in my mam's mind all the time, Mam did not question what she 'got up to' in the evenings!

I told Mam she was lying as she always did, but it did not stop Mam from believing her. Any money for birthdays or for me to have a new dress, which Mary took pleasure in making, was sent to her. She had changed her normal pattern of high neck and collar, to "cut across" shoulder to shoulder which did not suit me, so I never wore anything she made, but threw them away.

It upset me to think Mam believed her, and I told Mrs Powell how hurtful it was. She replied, "Well Kathleen, I think it is time I told you how your sister behaves, when you are on leave in Wales. She comes here, and says she needs to go up to your room. After a while, she comes down with several of your nice woollen jumpers and does not return them until you are due back from Wales."

I never challenged her about the woollies, although I was quite cross, but I told Mrs Powell, "Should she do the same thing again, whilst I am away, you have my authority to inform her, that I told you she was to stay out of my bedroom." The jumpers, I knitted myself, mostly complicated patterns, i.e. fan and feather stitch, cable or Fair Isle patterns, whilst sitting indoors with Mr and Mrs Powell; I also knitted fine lace gloves from a special "cotton", usually in blue, had a "frill cuff". Any "finishing off", I did by hand in the lunch time. I was unable to use a sewing machine, although Mrs Powell had a "treadle" machine; and it was available if I wished to use it.

Back in Holloway Institute, life went on as before, except that the tension between Barbara and Eileen spiralled; and Miss Clements suggested they

13

both calmed down. By lunch time, the girls split up, Barbara to her home, myself to look around and stretch my legs; Miss Laughey also left. Eileen stayed behind with Miss Clements as she usually did, and as it was not too nice a day to wander around; I returned to the office and surprised the pair of them! Sitting close together at a table were the two of them, they had a small glass tumbler and a Ouija board. They were having a "session with the departed", and Miss Clements was under her control, and that was Eileen's "shining glory".

After lunch, Eileen now started loosening her shoelaces, before proceeding to get her heels once more on Barbara's desk. I told Barbara to keep her cool; "Just pretend you haven't noticed what she is doing. Remove your inkwell beforehand and place it at the back of your typewriter, then once Eileen looks comfortable, knock the inkwell over her feet and legs!"

It worked, and Barbara, keeping a straight face, trying hard not to smile, told Eileen how sorry she was, and she hoped it had not stained her clothes; which it had; but it stopped Eileen from doing it again, and Barbara was unwinding at last!!

It wasn't Eileen's day, the afternoon tea break arrived and with the mugs on her fingers, she thumped her way downstairs to the second floor, but she fell the last few steps and hurt herself; so she said. As no-one left their desks to go and look! all the mugs with the exception of her own, were broken!!

One of the RAF lads from the telephone switchboard on that floor, dashed out to pick her up. He brought her back to the typing pool, all weepy, with her "shoelaces" undone: that was another habit she would have to discard.

I met one of the shiest lads that afternoon; his name was Leonard and he was walking out with Eileen at the time. I watched him call for her at 6 p.m. and she would raise one leg onto the desk at a time, and Leonard would tie her shoelace, then the second shoe and he repeated the chore! My sympathy went out to Leonard, he was a glutton for punishment. Possibly, had she been expelled from Mr George's Secretarial College early 1940, she may have changed her ways by now.

I met quite a few more girls from Trebanos and Ponty whilst in Stroud. Mabel Rock was in clerical, and she told me a good pal of mine named Ray Lewis had a position in Stroud Hospital as a nurse. We arranged to meet Ray after her shift one evening, and so we both waited outside the front of the hospital, and we saw Ray; up went the window and we shouted "Have you been busy?"

To which she replied quite loudly "I'm on Men's Ward, and I've been shaving 'cocks' all day!!"

Ray was a tonic, she had blonde hair, Marilyn Monroe looks and figure;

she was a natural. She never showed off — she just kept us "in fits" each time we met, and she brought us up-to-date with hospital escapades! Definitely a tonic to any patient coming out of anaesthetic; one look at Ray when he'd wake up, would be the 'lift-up' he needed!!

Phyllis Williams from Ponty, was in clerical also. She was a fair deal older than I was and had worked in "Jenkins Cash Stores" the grocers in lower Herbert Street. She was 'better off' monetarily, but had no qualifications with regard to office work. It did seem unfair of the Air Ministry, not to take into account one's qualifications.

Back in the office, days came and went as always, notifying parents about their sons or fathers. The Duke of Kent was one on my list, although he was killed in an accident over Scotland; and the Duchess of Kent, informed us, she did not wish to claim a pension.

Miss Clements asked me one day, what I did in the summer evenings? I told her apart from Saturday afternoons, when I came into Stroud and looked around, I did not go out in the evenings. She then told me, she and Mary Laughey liked to walk in the evenings, although not every evening, and she asked me, would I care to join them? My response was "Yes I would," and the following evening, the three of us slowly walked up to the Common, Rodborough Fort and roundabout. All the sights in the distance were pointed out to me. We seemed to like the same things and to unwind; and one could breathe fresher air.

I told her I would very much like to change my billet to get some more substantial food, I would still return to visit Mr and Mrs Powell. Miss Clements promised to look into it, but nothing ever happened.

The following Sunday was beautiful and sunny and I had been with Mr and Mrs Powell sometime. That morning, we both attended church and were just talking together; Mr Powell was in his usual chair near the fireplace smoking, when we heard lots of noisy footsteps coming down the cobbled side of Mrs Ersell's, and I was more than surprised to see my mam and dad and a friend named Lynis Rees, who had brought them up to see me in his van. I cannot quite remember whether my young sister was with them. They were together about two to three hours with Mr and Mrs Powell. I took Lynis up to the church and showed him the local village and around the area.

Outside in the yard, Mam and Dad had their 'photo' taken with Mr and Mrs Powell, the ladies sitting and the men standing holding the back of the chair. Mrs Powell had told Mam what a nice girl I was, happy to spend evenings indoors playing cards, dominoes, or just sitting reminiscing times gone by. A different story to that which Mary was painting regularly in her letters home.

Lynis Rees, was a butcher's son from Alltwen, in his mid-thirties, and had a small butcher's shop next door to Jim Rengozzi's ice-cream parlour. He had asked me out a few times; once to the theatre in Swansea on an early closing day. I accepted and enjoyed the trip out. He was not my boyfriend, never was. Both his sisters, Peggy and Nesta I did know well and I liked them both. His younger sister was at Pontardawe Grammar and his brother "Phil", younger than he was, went with his girlfriend "Ina Morgan" to South Africa.

My first Christmas at home from the Air Ministry, Lynis met me as I came out of Neath Station around 7.30 p.m. The van was parked nearby. I was not expecting to see him, so I presumed Mam had told him; as he was calling at the house each week (she had given him one book for meat allowance). Anyway, I was glad to accept the 'lift' and get home quicker — but no, he turned the van into the front of his home in Alltwen where his parents ran a grocers/post office, and had large living accommodation; a four-bedroomed house, a large back yard and other outhouses.

He introduced me to his mother, and took my coat from me, when I said "I'm not staying, I need to get home."

He then took me to a large shed in the yard; it had several women in white coats, all plucking chickens for the Christmas orders. He said "I'll take you home later."

I sat there, I was furious and definitely not plucking chickens, I felt lousy and I was dressed in my best clothes.

I got up and went into the living room, where his mother said "The food will be ready soon."

I said "I don't want food, I was never coming here, I've been conned by your son, and I want to go home."

She said he would only go when he was ready.

I got home about 9.30 p.m., he dropped me off at the front gate and drove off! Mam was furious that I had stayed there. "Haven't you got a tongue in your head?" she asked.

I was not aware that he and Mam had fallen out some weeks before I came home, so he had deliberately been waiting at Neath Station to take me home, to annoy Mam. She then told me that he had been banned from visiting our house ever again. The row was to do with his pilfering Dad's best pyramid hankies from the sideboard drawer. Mam bought Dad half a dozen very nice handkerchiefs which he only used at weekends, or when he wore a suit. They were kept 'nicely laundered' in the drawer of the sideboard. However, six went down to five, then five went down to four, and poor Dad was told he was losing them, until Mam became suspicious, as Lynis Rees was the only caller during the week; delivering the meat.

16

She decided, the next visit he would make, she would excuse herself and tell him her purse was in the middle room; and from there she could watch every move going on by looking in the living room mirror by the back door. He immediately moved to the sideboard, took a handkerchief of Dad's, and put it in his pocket. Mam came out, accused him of stealing and was going to report him to the police. She told him to hand back the handkerchief and never to enter our home again!

I was soon to learn what a temper he had. I completely ignored him when on leave, and returning home one Saturday evening from the village, the light from the lamppost opposite our gate was out, for the first time ever; but I could make out the outline of his van by the gate. He released the handbrake and ran the van towards me. I jumped into the laurel hedge of the bottom garden, then got up and ran to the back door, but he got there before Mam could open it — as she always double locked the door at night. By now, I was on the floor, my head on the doorstep, and his hands were choking me.

Mam got the door undone, and in her hand she had a large poker. She told him to 'clear off' and that she would be reporting him to the police inspector — but he laughed at her, he said "They won't help you, we are 'well in' with the police."

The following week, a few days before returning to Stroud, around midday, I had to call at a house in Brecon Road between the small post office and the butchers (Desmond), so I kept to that side of the road. There was no pavement, and as I almost reached the butcher's shop, I saw a van (CTG 352) coming from Ynismeudw — I looked quickly around me, there was no traffic at all apart from the van driven by Lynis Rees. He put his foot on the accelerator and shot across the road deliberately to run me over. I was pinned against the wall just short of the shop. He got out and shouted at me angrily, "No matter how long it takes, or how far I have to go to find you — I shall kill you!"

I was trembling, I said "You're mad, like your father." He had described to me on one occasion, the family pet, a large dog like a Labrador, would not do, or did not do as his father wanted it to do, so his father "hung the dog"; and he laughed as he recounted the event.

His father was a heavily-built man, he had an extremely red face, as though he was about to break a "blood vessel". The type of man, you did not argue with. He was driving the meat van, having been to get the meat ration for themselves and customers, when he was stopped in Herbert Street near the "Roll of Honour" by a policeman, who was new to the village. The policeman, asked him to open the van, as he wanted to check the contents. His father said he had eleven sheep. The policeman made a note of it and his father got home quickly and hid four of the sheep in a special secret floor area outside. I presume they were dead!

Later, the suspicious policeman, being determined to carry out his job properly, returned to check once more. His father was adamant that the new constable was mistaken and only saw seven, but due to an impediment in his father's speech, it sounded like eleven. So he got away with it. The police station and the section house were supplied with all the meat they needed, so no doubt the new policeman got his marching orders, to keep his silence.

Travelling to and fro from the Air Ministry to Wales was not a long journey, possibly three and a half hours. On the return journey to Paddington, once the train had left Newport, we would slow down and stop, a small halt — sometimes could be fifteen minutes; at another platform on the opposite side of our platform, trains went to different destinations.

It was a very sunny day, I had a corner seat facing the front of our train. A large group of RAF officers, possibly thirty or more, stood in a tight circle waiting for theirs, and just as our train very slowly began to move forwards, they turned as one towards us. I was extremely shocked to see these young men were faceless, their eyes and nostrils were the only recognisable part of the rest of their face. It deeply saddened me and I thought often, what a lot of surgery these very young men had to follow, and more so, mental and physical anxiety and frustration.

Shortly after, returning again from a visit home, but on a later train, in the same area, our train stopped. It was pitch-dark, we were told leave the train, but wait on the small platform; we would eventually be picked up and join with the Paddington train. Air-raid sirens had sounded before our train had stopped. It was all hustle and bustle; people were panicking. Air Force personnel both male and female were getting separated, and looking for each other, as civilians did the same. The train must have been packed that night. The cold air, as I stood on that platform in the dark, made me shiver; one felt that any moment, something ghastly was going to happen; when someone in RAF uniform accidentally bumped into me, putting his arms on my shoulders, he said "I'm sorry, are you all right?"

I said "Yes, I'm all right — when I left Ponty I never dreamt I would be standing here with so many people."

"Ponty," he said, "I'm from Alltwen, my name is . . . . . Cotton!"

One of the Cotton brothers. Phyllis Williams was a girlfriend of one of them.

We decided to stay together, try and chat a little, take our minds off the delay. It lasted more than two hours before a smaller, relief train, took us

18

further on, and we parted, wishing each other good luck, keep safe.

Many nights whilst in Stroud, enemy aircraft were heard overhead. The air-raid siren would be heard, and the three of us would sit on the lower stairs for hours, wrapped up warmly. Although there were many RAF stations around us, the German bombers passed over and went further afield. Many times we sat on the lower stairs, for safety, only to be told by the neighbours we had heard the 'All Clear', and missed the alarm, and of course this gave them a laugh! One bomber did drop a bomb on the hillside, Selsey nearby — I believe in Lady Marling's grounds.

The following weekend, Miss Clements, Miss Laughey and myself, took the bus to Pairswick; one of the oldest, most picturesque villages near us. It had a beautiful church, surrounded by ninety-nine yew trees. The story goes, each time the hundredth tree was planted, it never grew! Visitors were everywhere, being a nice sunny day and we did find a small teashop on the main road, for home-made scones and cream; then back to Stroud and home.

On the Monday, Miss Clements asked me would I like a change and go over to the Subscription Rooms, as they were temporarily short staffed. Possibly it would be for four weeks at the most. There was no typing pool here, mainly clerical; various sections had their own supervisor or HCO and they would dictate letters to one of us shorthand typists. We had a small corner of a large room. The supervisor, Miss Randall, in charge of three of us, peered at me over her specs. I told her who I was, she said "You can sit near me," then silence.

A little later I needed an eraser, so I asked her "Could I borrow your rubber please?"

She said "Please do — I never have occasion to use it!!"

It was a relief to be doing something other than casualties, and I enjoyed the break, and also relief from the tantrums of Eileen, although strangely, she was to come into my life on many occasions, years later.

There was more activity outside Subscription Rooms and the rooms inside were brighter than Holloway Institute. Previously Subscription Rooms were used for concerts, including band concerts.

I told Miss Clements, that I would appreciate doing relief work any time, as long as it was no farther away from my billet; so, in no time, I was being sent to a very nice building, in the opposite direction, near Stonehouse. It was a ladies' college, before the Air Ministry commandeered it for 'the duration'. "Ryeford Hall" was a four-storey building situated on the left-hand side of the main road nearing Stonehouse. The gardens, the landscape, the hillside and all around, were beautiful.

Once again, we typists were at the top of the building. I arrived early on the Monday morning, and I was met by a senior civil servant; a permanent. Her name was Miss Dingle, a tall lady, extremely thin, dark short cropped hair, prominent eyes, again wearing spectacles, and a little unsteady on her feet; around thirty-five years of age. I could have burst out laughing.

She looked at me. "What's so funny?" she said.

I couldn't tell, I thought she looked like a "man in drag"! Had I known what a wonderful sense of humour this lady had, I might have done! and she would have walloped me! Her Christian name was Olive.

She said "Thank God you have come! I've been stuck on my own up here for the last month — they told me to go ahead and position the office desks, chairs, etc. Anyway it's great to see you," she said. "I suggest we two work in the same room, I'm expecting three more, and they can have the other room on the opposite side of the landing."

I said "It sounds fine to me, of course you're in charge."

As she moved around, I noticed she had a slight problem with her ankles. They were very prominent, and looked deformed, which made her walk with a slight gait as if she was unsteady or tipsy. She was aware of this and emphasised it by pulling funny faces at you.

I was going to suggest we find the tea things and have a 'cuppa', when she said, "Would you like a cuppa? I'll make you one."

I said "Oh yes please, I'll be the boss today and you'll be the boss tomorrow."

She hit me a friendly slap on the shoulder!

Although she had been there one month, it must have seemed more like three months, if you're alone. She had no work to do and boredom had set in.

I had got on with all the different people I worked with and settled in easily; but there was something here which made me feel I was on holiday and it was sometime before I realised what it was. Stroud had a large brewery, woollen mills and the stream; the town was busy. It was the overpowering smell of the hops, especially on a hot day — I felt I was suffocating. Here I could breathe clear air and the view from our office window was heavenly. The hillside and the landscape, King Stanley and Leonard Stanley, took one's breath away. Here too was a woollen mill and the stream which was used in the process of making the cloth. It was a steep walk to the top of the hill, and little cottages were dotted nearby for folk who worked at the woollen mill.

Mam sent money to Mary, so that both of us could have a new coat, and Mary suggested we go to Bon Marché in Gloucester. We had more or less dressed similarly as we grew up — this was now the time to change all that and so we found ourselves on this Saturday morning doing a "lot of looking before buying", and sure enough I found a beautiful silver grey coat, large collar and cuffs, padded shoulders and a long tie belt. I put it on, I looked in the mirror and I liked what I saw; besides, the coat was pure wool. I had been growing my hair longer than normal and was not sporting a "page boy" hairdo! With the belt tied as tight as I could, it gave me a nice figure, although I was still only eight stone. This coat, I was going to wear for weekends or trips home, definitely not the office. Mary had not made up her mind, but at the last moment, she chose the same coat as myself, then we left for the shuttle train back to our billets.

I was still with Mrs Powell, coming up to two years now, and I was surprised to find, when I got home, there was a letter for me, from Wales. I did not recognise the writing, so I went to my bedroom to read it. I was most surprised yet pleased to get the letter. It was from Mr Jones, the bachelor farmer, living in Trebanos; who had loaned my parents the money to buy "Raglan House". They had what one would call a 'Welsh mortgage!".

From time to time, he would visit and take whatever sum of money Mam had managed to save. There were no set rules. He deducted this amount from the loan and returned the book to Mam. He was about my father's age, extremely shy, and most of his time he spent on the farm. His sister was married and she and her husband lived with him. They too, had a 'milk round', and we passed it in Trebanos, as we were on our way home to Pen-Y-Graig and there was always a cheery greeting to each other as they held their whips up high. I believe the brother-in-law was named Hughes.

Mam always asked Mr Jones to stay to tea, which was set out in the middle room on the large table. A nice ham salad, followed by home-made tart or cake. He always sat opposite me, his back to the fire, and I was always warned beforehand by Mam, not to embarrass him, as this made him drop his knife or fork! All I did was "wink" at him if he caught my eye! I did not think there was any harm in that!

Here he was now, writing to ask me how I was getting on, and telling me, that he had called at Raglan House a few times, and he missed seeing me! "You were always full of fun," he wrote.

I answered his letter, and I told him it was hard work; 9 a.m. until 6 p.m. Mondays to Fridays, and I could have welcomed some of that "ham salad!". I thanked him for writing and I wished him well.

The second letter was even more of a surprise, he explained he had worked hard farming, from a young age, but now, he was thinking more and more, that perhaps he should settle down.

I thought 'Are you referring to me?' So I sent the letter home to Mam and Dad, who told me not to encourage him. He may be wealthy, but I could end up working my fingers off!

However, on my next leave, I heard he was seriously ill with pneumonia, and on Mam's advice, we both got the bus to Trebanos Cross, and walked all the way up to the farm. It was dark when we got there, and he was 'tucked-up' in bed in his striped flannel nightshirt. He was embarrassed to see us, so we left early after telling him to get well soon.

Apparently, the following day, he got out of bed, insisting he felt better, but was not, and returned to the fields to work. A few days later, he died of double pneumonia. We later learned, he was a very wealthy man. It turned out, he owned more than half the village of Trebanos!

Before the month was up, the rest of the "expected staff" had arrived for the typing pool, at Ryeford Hall. The first, was an Australian lady, similar age to Miss Dingle. She had worked for a shipping company in London, and was now directed to "work of importance" (the war effort) and thus we were to enrich ourselves by having Audrey in our office. We loved her from the moment she chose where to sit, near the window, as she was to be 'Top Secretary', although she was a temporary civil servant at the time. She would need all the light she could get; if she was to work nonstop, as she did; being in great demand for shorthand by most of the heads of departments. The fastest typist I ever saw; a touch typist. We decided to call her 'Aussie'. Her thick dark hair curled around her sun-tanned face, her eyes were "doe like" and she would "roll" them if you told her anything you thought may have been of interest to her. She looked hypnotised, she could make her eyes grow larger and larger, of course, this was part of Aussie's character — she too, was full of fun!

Aussie was billeted at the top of the hill, with a Miss Sellars, a lady who owned a farm, which we could see from our window. She went home to lunch each working day. She always wore a woollen headscarf tied under her chin, a heavy woollen cape, in bold checks of beige, brown and black, and her shoes; 'brown suede flatties'! We felt sorry for her, pushing her bicycle to the top of the hill, but, coming down, it was freewheel — and whoever saw her first, would shout "Here she comes" and with the wind under her cape — she looked like a huge bat, flying down the hill, or the wicked witch on her broom!!

Of course, we took our turn in teasing her, but she would put her 'tongue out' at us, and say "Ah! But I've just had a gorgeous meal — worth pushing my bike for, and you both — you're jealous!" She was a treasure and we were both pleased she was with us. Her full name was Audrey Gertrude Salamonson; and in the morning when signing in the register, there was never enough room for all her name, so she was allowed to enter A. G. Salamonson.

Air Ministry rules were very strict, we all signed the Secrets Act, and there were signs around aplenty 'Keep Mum', 'Careless Talk Costs Lives', and so on. Aussie had many troubles which she overcame alone. She regularly saved holiday time to visit her mother who was in a nursing home, crippled with arthritis, and a long journey entailed to visit her. Her mother wrote to her regularly also, and Aussie would show us her mother's handwriting. It was almost 'script' like, it was beautiful. She loved her mother dearly. She had married a soldier, who was a Dutchman. He had been constantly in trouble, and every time she drew her army allowance, it was put in a registered envelope and posted to him. It was what he expected. He gave her nothing in return, and I believe she was frightened of him.

One afternoon, there sounded some excitement on one of the lower floors. Our extension phone rang and Aussie was asked to come down at once. She returned almost immediately, picked up her coat, etc., and left with her husband. No one who saw him knew who he was, except that he was tall, smart and a film star type.

Aussie arrived the following morning, none of us asked any questions and Aussie never mentioned anything. We knew it was better that way.

Aussie asked me one morning during our tea break whether I would like a "penfriend". She told me he was a soldier serving in Gibraltar, and would welcome a letter from a penfriend back home. She had worked with him in the shipping company, Lep Transport. They shipped livestock, both wild and domestic worldwide. His name was Jack. Aussie laughed as she told me Jack was taking some miniature Shetland ponies to the docks for shipment to a Rajah in India. They were for his children's coaches. It was Armistice Day 1938 and Jack and his boss heard the maroon go off and they stood to attention — unfortunately Jack had his back to a pony who raised his tail and deposited a 'packet' on the back of his new overcoat! As well as livestock he also dealt with imports of wool, mainly from Czechoslovakia, transported through Germany — one day he was told by the city wool merchant to look for a 'bale' with peculiar markings. When he spotted it, the customs officer was called over and on opening it, they saw masses of jewellery and gold coins; the whole wealth of a Jewish family escaping from the Nazis.

I wrote a few lines to Jack in Gibraltar; mainly my age, interests, my home town, then I was called out for shorthand; so it would be lunch time before I could add a little more. However, I could not find this scrap of paper which was to be the basis of my first letter to Jack, so I waited for Aussie to return "on her broomstick" only to be told, she had taken the piece of paper, enclosed it with her letter and put it in the mail room. Nothing was allowed out of the mail room, once it had gone in for posting. So now of course I had a 'penfriend'!!

I soon received a letter from Jack together with a pair of pure silk stockings and a promised photo which he hoped would not be mistaken for a 'Rock Ape'. Furthermore, a friend whose ship had recently docked at Gibraltar, would be posting me a further present. It was a beautiful French lipstick by Guerlain; all the girls were now begging for "pen pals". Strangely, amongst the lads serving on the Rock, was a headmaster's son from the next village to Pontardawe — Rhydyfro. His name was Alan Terry. He had a sister, Margaret.

We were still awaiting the two remaining staff, to bring us up to five. They were due at any time we were informed, although dear Aussie kept the workload down, by taking it on herself. The two girls arrived about the same time but from different parts of the country. They were two opposites, and as arranged by Miss Dingle — they had the room on the opposite of the landing.

June, the younger, was tall, attractive, with dark shoulder length curly hair. She lived close to Ryeford Hall; her father also worked in our building. He was an HCO (Higher Clerical Officer), and the family had leased a nice bungalow just ten minutes from the office, for the duration of hostilities. Mr Terry was in charge of a large section of clerical workers and each morning would see him smartly attired (Anthony Eden's double), arriving for work; with attaché case and rolled umbrella. June, knew she was attractive and she swanned around, a lump of chewing gum in her mouth; continually addressing us as "Say Kid!!", and so on.

Her colleague was Olwen, or "Ollie" as we christened her. She was from Newport (near Cardiff). Her parents had died when she was a schoolgirl, and she was brought up by her older sister and husband. They had certainly done a good job of it. She was short, a natural blonde, hair parted in the middle, with full cherry-lipped mouth, and large bright eyes.

Nothing could have been better. We all liked each other and we got on very well. At least I did, I was in with the two comedians, "Ding" and "Auss" and there was no stress here at all.

The work here for us was: Airmen's Pay Ledgers and Accounts.

Chapter Three

Making Friends in Stroud

The following Saturday, Mary told me she was to get some material to make me a dress. Again, Mam had sent her the money; so in the afternoon, we both walked into Stroud, wearing our new coats. As we arrived there, the rain got heavier, but we managed to get to the shop before being too wet.

In the doorway of the shop, which had "display windows" on either side, were two airmen sheltering from the rain. They smiled at us as we went inside the shop. They both looked nice, clean and smart. One was tall and blond, the other shorter, thickset with dark hair.

I had already told Mary I did not want her making me any more clothes. What she was making now was "old-fashioned"; the material she chose was what older ladies wore in Mam's days. A dark material with a raised pattern in the material; I believe the name was "cloqué".

I kept looking towards the doorway and the lads were smiling at me. She paid for the material, handed over the clothing coupons, then told me, "Don't look at those airmen, they will think we are tarts!"

By now the rain was heavy again, and she decided not to wait until it stopped, but to dash across to Woolworth's stores, and get lost in the crowd. It was a large store with counters displaying various wares.

We had our heads down, trying to hide from these airmen, when a voice over my shoulder said "How would you like a feather for you hat?"

Well, we hadn't even noticed the counter had a display of various feathers; I almost choked, as I was wearing a grey pure 'Angora' forage cap, held on one side of my head by a long hat pin at least four inches long with a striped black and white knob on the end. Even Mary laughed.

The lads said "How about going outside to have a chat? The rain has stopped!"

She exploded "We are not tarts or pick-ups, so don't waste your time!"

However, once outside, we saw the funny side — they were both at

Aston Down Aerodrome, five miles uphill from Stroud. They again asked us if we would like to go for a walk.

Mary said "No, definitely not."

They both looked serious and the tall one asked "What about next Saturday afternoon then? We will be here in front of Woolworths!"

She said "All right."

My airman was named Charles and came from Cowbridge in Lincolnshire. Mary's airman was named Johnny Wood; he was a solicitor's clerk and came from Surrey, I believe.

The following Saturday I walked into Stroud, I did not go with her or see her there, but Charles was on his own and I presumed she had gone into Stroud before me.

Charles asked me what I would like to do. I said "Well, at this moment, I would love a 'cuppa' and something to eat. I'm starving!"

He took me to Gloucester Road (near the police station) and we went into the local café. He seemed to know the owner and asked him to cook me something special. There was a small corner balcony on the second floor, room for two or three tables and I sat there about ten minutes before a plateful of fish, chips and peas was brought; followed by home-made tart and custard. I ate it all and felt better immediately.

Charles joined me for a cup of tea — he was smiling and said "Feel better?"

I said "Yes, thanks. It's almost two years since I had as much food as that and it feels lovely."

We then left, and went to the early show at the cinema near Woolworths. Once inside, he bought me a box of chocolates saying "Get those down you"! Of course I had no room for anything more and I thanked him. With our tickets I found we were sitting upstairs in the balcony and he was a non-smoker, so we huddled together, he with his arm around my shoulder, and watched the film. He did not speak, but now and again he hugged my shoulder close.

After the film, it was still early evening, so we took a walk to Stratford Park, not too far away. It was a beautiful park and we sat and talked, giving each other a little information about ourselves.

I told him how long I had been in Stroud at the Air Ministry, full stop! And how I longed to find a new billet where I got some food.

He was quite alarmed to hear how little food I got, whereas he was a farmer's son and the food at the base was ample, but not always their favourite, so when he went home on leave, they always made sure they "killed the fatted calf"!! Turkey/pork normally.

I also told him I now had a 'penfriend'; we recently started writing to each other; he was in Gibraltar.

26

He told me he had a 'girlfriend' back home named Dorothy and both parents kept asking them when they were going to name the day; as they had been going together quite some time. We both felt we wanted to meet again, so we told each other we would be good friends, we would enjoy each other's company and keep dating. After asking me when we could meet, I thought Tuesday evenings and Saturdays, for the whole day.

The Tuesday evenings about 7 p.m., he would walk to Cainscross and meet me halfway from my billet. From then, it was straight to the café, then either a nice walk or the cinema. I never saw Mary out with John, but she was seeing him, as Charles told me Johnny had a date! I don't know where she went; at least now, she left me alone and that was sheer heaven!

The summer evenings were so enjoyable, we never stopped chatting. I really looked forward to our meetings; of course there were breaks, when he went home on leave; then I would eagerly look forward to his return, when he surprised me with a nicely wrapped package.

The park was nearby, so we would get seated, and when I "opened the package", there were beautiful large slices of lean turkey, his mother had packed for him to bring back. I did not know whether he had mentioned me and how I never had much food to eat, as the following leave pass, saw him with the second package for me. This time, it was delicious slices of roast port.

How kind he was, and I was beginning to feel a lot better, the gnawing stomach pains I experienced for so long were easing off, and besides, I was earning just a few shillings more each week, and could afford to go for a "British restaurant" meal, which was one shilling (5p); once or twice a week.

The girls in the office, June and Ollie, were full of chat. Ollie had met a smart, nice-looking soldier, named Robert Carrol, stationed nearby on the outskirts of Stonehouse, so she rode her bicycle each working day, to talk to "Bobby" in her lunch time. She had met the only man she would ever be interested in. He came from South Shields, and she adored him from the start. Whilst I was at Ryeford Hall, she became engaged to him.

June, on the other hand, seventeen years of age, could have told us "oldies", all one needed to know about "blokes" — she was 'boy mad' and I believe a bit of a worry to her parents. She had a younger sister about twelve years of age. She was lovely but going through the embarrassing stage of having to wear a 'brace' on her top teeth; so she shyly covered her mouth with her hand. I told her she would have beautiful teeth once the brace came off, and it would be worthwhile.

As Christmas was getting nearer, I wondered whether Mrs Powell would perhaps manage to get some poultry and make a nice meal. I need not have raised such hopes, as my name was drawn "out of the hat", for "skeleton staff" duty on Christmas day.

Before I left for the office, she gave me something for lunch. It was a miniature tin of pink salmon (half the size of a small tin today) and a few tablespoons of dry potato powder.

I arrived at the office, the usual time, the building seemed empty. The telephone was 'put through' to my office, to take any calls. I would not have been able to deal with any, as I worked solely with APL (Airmen's Pay Ledgers). I was to make a note of the "caller" and the extension number needed.

Around 11 a.m., I was aware of footsteps downstairs. It was eerie; a four-storey building and just myself on the top floor with creeping 'goose pimples'. The footsteps were heavy and coming higher and nearer; someone was already on the second floor by now. I could scream, but who would hear me? There was talk about the old night watchman, who tried your door handles when you were on fire duty. Make sure you 'lock your door', others had advised; but Christmas day? No, it would not be him. I knew as the footsteps reached the third floor, I had to do something. I had to be ready to throw something of weight; if I was in danger. Then the footsteps stopped on the top step of the fourth floor, and "joy of joys", there stood Mr Terry, June's father. He smiled at me and told me the family planned to have Christmas dinner — late afternoon, and would I please join them, they would be delighted if I would; and he would see me home safely, to my billet late evening, in Cainscross. I told him, they were most kind, I would love to join them; and meet the rest of the family.

It was a Christmas I will always remember; a lovely dinner, games and chats through the evening and invitations to call on them any time. "Please feel one of the family."

I reached home around 9.30 p.m. Mr Terry saw me safely down the side of Mrs Ersell's, as that side of the cottages was closed in. It was 'pitch-dark' and had been known for some strangers to shelter or court there.

My eyes took in the scene as I opened the door. There sat Mr and Mrs Powell with their friends, Mr and Mrs Lovejoy and their son, an RAF cadet, playing cards. The butler sink was laden-up with dishes and saucepans, and the remains of a large turkey nearby.

Mr Powell remarked, "Lass will soon make short work of those dirty dishes in the sink, won't you lass?"

I went to my room to have an early night. I felt choked, and unkindly commented, "Not me, I did not dirty them." I wondered later, if he could get a turkey for Christmas, why did he not bring home the odd chicken or so for Sunday?

I could never get to the bottom of my billet problem. Why could I not get transferred to younger people. Then one day, all was made clear to me. The Air Ministry never billeted staff with anyone over fifty years of age. Also, if you did not find your billet through the Air Ministry, they were not concerned with your problems, and on the whole, all billets they chose for staff would be looked into if you were unhappy, and a second billet found for you.

This was the case with Mary. Originally when Mary joined the Air Ministry, after Mam answered their advertisement in the paper; she was sent to a beautiful college for girls in Westonbirt, Wiltshire. She was billeted with other girls outside but was unhappy because of the atmosphere amongst the girls; so she asked to be given employment somewhere different. The Air Ministry stepped in immediately, transferred Mary to Gloucester, at the Meteorological Office and found her the billet next door but one to Mrs Powell with a lady in her thirties; (Mrs Parsloe). Here she was never short of food; there being full rations and Mrs Parsloe was young enough to dash around for the odd bits and bobs, i.e. fish off the ration; when the word got around. What Mary had done, was to ask Mrs Powell whether she could take me in, so that she could keep an eye on me, just two doors away. She never told or asked Mrs Powell to feed me. Normally the guinea per week paid from your wages per week, which your landlady drew from the post office on an allowance book, was meant to feed you *and* sleep you. More than possibly, Mrs Powell was doing very well; thinking the guinea was for sleeping; and it would tally with me never seeing the table laid for a meal for the three of us at any time. They ate meals different times between 9 a.m. and 6 p.m., and I ate the same evening meal, a large plate of porridge with treacle on top; each working day.

Of course I wrote home to Mam and told her I was starving, but Mary when questioned by Mam, told her, "She is so fussy with her food, she would *push it away* — sausages, pies, meat of different sorts. She would strongly stress to Mrs Powell, 'I'm not eating that'!" I was being very difficult? I lived in no. 3, Mary in no. 1.

So Mam started sending me occasionally a large jam sandwich. I would take it to my room and eat the lot! Mam made it with liquid paraffin.

I thought for a while I would go for a bedsit, near the office. One guinea per week; feed yourself. At least I would have my ration book and points to myself. There was no other way out. Then, Charles came back from leave, and of course, he made sure I was never hungry — he was so concerned, there was always the pub for a change, but he did not suggest it. He always joined his mates from the camp during the week, at the same pub when not seeing me. They travelled back to camp in vehicles laid on. After 11 p.m. — you had to walk the five miles, and he always did when he saw me.

As summer evenings changed to autumn, the evening temperature got colder, and walks with it. We would wrap up well, but still you were never warm.

Mrs Powell surprised me one evening as I left to meet Charles. She said "Don't you stay out long tonight now or you'll catch your death of cold. It's a moonlight night but also bitterly cold." She continued . . . "You are very welcome to bring your young man home you know. He may like to visit, will you ask him?" I promised to do that.

When I asked Charles, he was delighted and our next meeting was at no. 3. The doorbell rang at the front door. I dashed up the stairs to let him in, taking his overcoat from him. Down the stairs he came, a big grin on his face, and they were both quite excited.

Mr Powell almost shook his hand off. "Nice to see you," he said. "Beat you double top."

Then Mrs Powell joined in the darts game and jolly good she was at it.

From then it became a regular weekly visit and I could see they used to look forward to him coming. Mrs Powell praised me and said how much they liked me, nice to have someone in the house, etc., and they both thought Charles an extremely nice young man, and told me so. He could call any time he wished.

Things were beginning now to become livelier at the office. We were in charge of Airmen's Pay Ledgers and had records of all the lads at Aston Down. Girls meeting airmen in the evenings and going out with them, would buzz in, then ask us whether we would tell them if Private .... or Corporal .... or Sergeant .... was married? All we needed was rank, name and number, then we would check, and I only found one who was not married, and claiming child allowance! Yes only one! So I checked up Johnny Wood and found he was married. Charles was LAC C. Sykes and single.

Soon after this, Mary was being extremely rude to me, so it gave me great pleasure in telling her, "Well, at least I don't go out with married men!"

She exploded, and replied "And neither do I" followed by the "queen of slaps" and my face was swollen for the whole day. Anyway she was engaged to Desmond and should have known better!

Back in the office, news that Ollie was taking instruction to change to the Catholic faith did not surprise us. Her and "Bobby" were going to get married fairly soon. I was very pleased for her. Again, she asked me to give up my billet but as Charles was allowed to come and spend evenings with us at no. 3, I refrained.

June was "out on the town" with different lads, each one was "smashing kid", why don't you come and make a foursome? It did not appeal to me.

"Ding" we found, was spending some lunch hours, walking out with a

30

chap from clerical. He was much older than Ding — and he wore a long shabby gabardine Mackintosh, no matter what the weather was like. They normally walked along the main road to Stonehouse and back. He was a 'shady' type of chap; so whilst tormenting one another one day, I said to Ding, "Are you serious with your gentleman friend?"

She said "Why do you ask?"

"Well, I wondered how he would be able to kiss you, if you wanted to?"

"Oh! that's no problem" she said, "you see, we've got a bucket hidden in the grounds for such occasions and when he wants a kiss, I put the bucket on my head and he swings up on the handle!"

Daft question. Silly answer!

The lady who cleaned the offices would arrive before 6 p.m. A plump motherly lady, round faced, although a trifle shy. She would clean the stairs and landings first and wait until we left, before doing the office. She was a widow with two daughters; they worked in the woollen mills nearby. She told me, she also had a son, named Jack, he did most of the housework, also the washing, because he could not do work away from the cottage. Her name was Mrs Swales, she was lucky, she said, to get the job at Ryeford Hall. We all liked her, but she kept busy and never wasted time. We could also see her cottage from our window.

She stopped me, one evening, and said she would like me to come and have lunch with them one Wednesday, and meet her family. She had been telling them about me, being similar age to the girls.

I accepted her invitation and met the girls, who had only a short break for lunch, so the meal was served straight away. Her son Jack, was in the yard, wringing the washing through an enormous wooden mangle, his face one big smile, but his poor body was badly deformed; an enormous lump on his back and one leg crippled. Mentally he was unblemished, spoke with a good sense of humour, and sat beside me. We got on fine and he kept me in fits of laughter.

My plate was full of dinner — liver, bacon and vegetables, followed by suet pudding with 'home-made' jam. It was delicious and I thanked her for the kindness. We still had time for a chat before leaving for the office. She asked me, would I join them every Wednesday for lunch from then on; the lunch would always be liver, bacon, etc.

She could also get me woollen cloth from the mill at great reductions, as the girls were entitled to buy at a discount.

I said, I would write to my mam, so perhaps she would get me some samples of cloth with the price per yard. This she would do she said, and I sent them home to Mam. Pure West of England cloth at a fraction of the normal price. Mam wrote back, telling me how much material I would need for a costume allowing some extra for the pattern if the suit was pleated at all. I was to choose two suit lengths (no coupons for material necessary as one would — if buying from a shop). The money she enclosed with the letter, plus an extra couple of pounds for her kindness. I said I doubt if she would accept anything for herself, so Mam said "Then give it to Jack, her son." Also, perhaps she knew of some tailor who could make up the two costumes? One length was "Prince of Wales check", the other a beautiful "shade of terracotta"!

I found a tailor and tailoress near Stratford Park. They were recommended to me. Husband and wife, they were German Jewish refugees. I called at the address given to me and found their workroom at the top of the house. They knew exactly the style of costume I wanted, and said it was a delight to work on good material.

Mam paid all the costs. I was 'over the moon'. This was the first time she had ever trusted me with the necessary money. I kept the two costumes at home, they were too nice for work.

Ollie informed us she was taking a couple of weeks' leave and with Bobby, went to his home and from there, got married. She glowed, and we were all happy for her.

I was now getting regular letters from Jack in Gibraltar, and in them, he would tease Aussie! "Don't believe all those tales the 'abos' tell you!" She also got letters and would relate some of the escapades he got up to at the shipping company! She told me that Jack had to go to the Royal Albert Docks to collect two snakes (boa constrictors) from a boat. He thought he would make a few shillings, so, instead of using a taxi from the docks, he caught a no. 15 bus which went to the Mansion House. He put the two "pigeon carriers" under the stairs and the conductor said, "I can't hear the cooing!" Jack told him, "I'll show you the birds when you help me off the bus."

Outside the Mansion House, with the containers on the pavement, Jack lifted the lids and showed the eight foot and six foot boa constrictors! The conductor went as white as a ghost, he leapt back onto the platform and banged the bell at least six times and it sped off!!

Another day, Jack's boss, Mr Haase, a New Zealander, sent Jack to collect a goat from a Romanian boat. It was an expensive rare breed on its way to a millionaire collector in Chicago. Jack paid extra for a taxi driver to take them to Upper Thames Street. The goat stunk, so Jack opened the taxi windows wide.

Everything was all right until they reached Bishopgate, where a police constable had his arm outstretched to hold traffic up, and the horrible goat put his head 'out of the window' and grabbed the policeman's tunic by the cuff and pulled the arm of the coat right out!!

The author at seventeen

My pen friend

'His' pen friend

Hilly Orchard and Canal, Cainscross

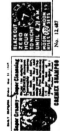

Daily Express

No. 12,467 — Friday, May 31, 1940 — One Penny

Through an inferno of bombs and shells the B.E.F. is crossing the Channel from Dunkirk—in history's strangest armada

TENS OF THOUSANDS SAFELY HOME ALREADY

Many more coming by day and night

SHIPS OF ALL SIZES DARE THE GERMAN GUNS

UNDER THE GUNS OF THE BRITISH FLEET, UNDER THE WINGS OF THE ROYAL AIR FORCE, A LARGE PROPORTION OF THE B.E.F. WHO FOR THREE DAYS HAD BEEN FIGHTING THEIR WAY BACK TO THE FLANDERS COAST, HAVE NOW BEEN BROUGHT SAFELY TO ENGLAND FROM DUNKIRK.

Fleet to return were the wounded. An armada of ships of all sizes and shapes—were used for crossing the Channel. The weather which helped Hitler's tanks to advance has since helped the British evacuation.

Cost to the Navy of carrying out, in an inferno of bombs and shells, one of the most magnificent operations in history has been three destroyers, some auxiliary craft, and a small steamer.

Cost to the enemy of the Fleet's intervention outside Dunkirk can be counted in the shattering of German advanced forces by naval guns and the use ...

Tired, dirty, hungry they came back —unbeatable

By HILDE MARCHANT

THREE DESTROYERS LOST
As Navy helps B.E.F.

Signposts to be removed

Gracie goes to America

WITH a rod, stroke and ...

STOP PRESS

FRENCH SAVE PLANES FOR COUNTER ATTACK
—Russian Report.

SIR JOHN REITH, Minister of Transport announced last night that "airways authorities ...

Daily Express, *31st May, 1940 — George safe*

News Chronicle

No. 29,564   WEDNESDAY, MAY 28, 1941   RADIO PAGE 2   •   ONE PENNY

BISMARCK: THE FIRST FULL STORY

Air and Sea Chase Lasted Four Days, Covered 1,750 Miles

Churchill Gives News From Bits Of Paper

CANADIAN PLANES CAME FROM NEWFOUNDLAND | **A FLEET SAILED UP FROM GIBRALTAR**

FROM THE ADMIRALTY AND THE AIR MINISTRY THERE CAME LAST NIGHT THE FIRST FULL ACCOUNT OF THE FOUR DAYS OF ATLANTIC BATTLE AND PURSUIT WHICH CULMINATED AT 11.1 A.M. YESTERDAY IN THE SINKING OF THE BISMARCK, FINEST FIGHTING SHIP IN HITLER'S FLEET.

NEXT TWO DAYS ARE VITAL IN BATTLE FOR CRETE

From BERTHA GASTER

CAIRO, Tuesday.

1,000 Saved from Ships Lost In Battle of Crete

ON PAGE TWO

Greatest Sea v. Air Battle in History. By One Who Was There.

The End of the Bismarck. By Maj. Fielding Eliot

ROOSEVELT SPEAKS

News Chronicle, *28th May, 1941 — My birthday surprise*

OFFICIAL PAID

MINISTRY OF FOOD

RATION BOOK
SUPPLEMENT

This is a Spare Book

YOU WILL BE TOLD
HOW AND WHEN TO USE IT

HOLDER'S NAME AND REGISTERED ADDRESS

Surname..........*HERRING*

Other Names.........*William R*

Address.........*1 Walton Way*
.........*Mitcham*

NATIONAL REGISTRATION NO.

| CNCZ | 37 | 1 |

Class and Serial No. of Ration Book already held
KBI PP 609997

If found, please return to

MITCHAM
FOOD OFFICE
9 JUL 1941

Date of Issue:

R.B. 9

NATIONAL REGISTRATION
IDENTITY
CARD

Typical identity card and ration book

T.S. 1/62—McC & Co Ltd—51-4662

MEMORANDUM.

Sender's Reference	Receiver's Reference	Date
* O1/xhir/ME/197	*	14. AUG. 43.

TO: OFFICER. COMMANDING.
68. MEDIUM. RGT. RA.

No. 1444394. W/Bdr. DURRAN T. J. K.

The attached proforma in lieu of AFB
2634 in respect of the a/n NCO is
forwarded to you for retention.
Whilst serving in Battalion this
NCO was considered to be potential
OCTU Candidate.

Letter re Jack as OCTU candidate

An engaged couple

Wedding — 18th December, 1943

SUPREME HEADQUARTERS
ALLIED EXPEDITIONARY FORCE

Soldiers, Sailors and Airmen of the Allied Expeditionary Force!

You are about to embark upon the Great Crusade, toward
which we have striven these many months.   The eyes of
the world are upon you. The hopes and prayers of liberty-
loving people everywhere march with you. In company with
our brave Allies and brothers-in-arms on other Fronts,
you will bring about the destruction of the German war
machine, the elimination of Nazi tyranny over the oppressed
peoples of Europe, and security for ourselves in a free
world.

Your task will not be an easy one. Your enemy is well
trained, well equipped and battle-hardened. He will
fight savagely.

But this is the year 1944 ! Much has happened since the
Nazi triumphs of 1940-41. The United Nations have in-
flicted upon the Germans great defeats, in open battle,
man-to-man.   Our air offensive has seriously reduced
their strength in the air and their capacity to wage
war on the ground. Our Home Fronts have given us an
overwhelming superiority in weapons and munitions of
war, and placed at our disposal great reserves of trained
fighting men.   The tide has turned ! The free men of the
world are marching together to Victory !

I have full confidence in your courage, devotion to duty
and skill in battle. We will accept nothing less than
full Victory !

Good Luck ! And let us all beseech the blessing of Al-
mighty God upon this great and noble undertaking.

Dwight D Eisenhower

General Eisenhower's message to troops

1464394 Bdr. Jack Durrant
68 Med Regt RA
LM Coy
42 RHU.
Aldershot.

My Own Darling,

Just a few more rushed
lines my darling — to ask you
not to write to me at this
address anymore. Will let
you have my new address as
soon as possible. The next few
days for me will be both
anxious & exciting & I will
write as soon as possible
darling

Oh. Kath. darling I do
love you so very much and
will be so glad when we
win this ruddy war and I
can return to you my darling
— this time for good!

Please don't worry too much
darling! I promise I'll
take no chances and will

Part of letter to me on the message

My friend Lieutenant George A. Altass — Killed on invasion

No.D3/W30HO Cas/D/ .... FORM B. 104—81A
(If replying, please quote
above No.)

.... Record Office,

....19

S̶i̶r̶ ̶o̶r̶ MADAM

     I regret to have to inform you that a report has been received from the
War Office to the effect that (No.) _1HHH39H_

(Rank) _W/Bdr (Art/Clerk)_

(Name) _Jack DURRANT_

(Regiment) _Royal Artillery (Field)_

has been wounded, and was admitted to _Hospital_

not reported

on the _16th_ day of _April_ 1945 The

nature of the wound is _Facial burns and injury to ey_
Western Europe

    I am to express to you the sympathy and regret of the Army Council.

    **Any further information received at his office as to his
condition will be at once notified to you.**

        Yours faithfully,

        JHWoodhead

          Officer in Charge of Records

IMPORTANT.—Any change of address should be immediately notified to this Office.

(8360) *M10452/2579 7/44 103m (6) JC&S 702   Forms/B 104—81A/3

Notice informing me that Jack was wounded

My husband in Germany

Jack and I in retirement

The police constable arrested Jack, the goat and the taxi driver and took them all to Bishopsgate Police Station, where an inspector telephoned Mr Haase, and he agreed to buy a new jacket for the policeman!

The many holidays I spent at home, were normally a week at a time; I never told them I was coming, but would turn up to surprise them, and in doing this, I believe I was more help each time I arrived home.

On one occasion, it was midday, I got home to find the whole table covered in jars and bottles of preserves from the pantry. Mam was going to give the pantry a whitewash! She looked at me and said, "I would not have this lot on the table, had I known you were coming."

So I said, "Tell you what — you make me a nice 'cup of tea', I'll change my clothes and I'll whitewash the pantry. How's that for your lucky day?"

She said "Would you?"

Of course I would!

Whereas I was continually being reminded by Mary that she always wrote and told them when she would be arriving; so that they could expect her!

On another unannounced visit, I noticed a load of coal had been unloaded at the back of the coal house, "on the right-of-way path". Dad was working and was not due home for a few hours, so I stripped off my best clothes and donned some old ones, then went outside and shovelled it through the small door, down into the coal house. It was hard work, tiring, but each shovelful in, was one less left to do; and I managed to clear the lot. I was brushing the 'pathway' when Dad arrived, out of breath; he looked annoyed. I explained, "I thought it would help if I did this for you, after working your shift, you don't want to start again here."

He took my hand in his, he said "You will ache all over after doing this, whereas, I wouldn't, as I'm shovelling coal every shift. You are a good girl, you meant well, but don't do it again."

A nice bath and shampoo soon made me look more myself, but he was right, I ached all over.

During this particular week, I had taken a walk to the village, hoping to see Una my friend, and as I walked along Brecon Road towards the bus garage, a young man my age, was smiling at me before I had reached him. He was waiting for his bus home. His hair was still curly, although he looked frail, his cheeks were highly coloured.

He said "How are you Kathleen? It is years since we have seen each other, although I have often thought about you."

It had to be Trebanos, and the only boyfriend I had there, was Lewis

33

Lewis, who shared my warm cakes when I was at cookery class! He was laughing — we were so young and innocent. He had a brother and twin brothers. He was the eldest of the four. His father was a postman in Trebanos.

He told me, he had just come out of the sanatorium, where he had spent a long time, but now he was discharged; no doubt he would get stronger. I prayed he would too. It broke my heart to hear he 'passed away' a short time after we met; but happy to have met him again and find a bond still there of our closeness at the cookery/manual classes held on the Graig. We were both possibly nine years old.

I did not see Una, as I had hoped; she had become a driver on ARP Heavy Disposal Unit. She already had a driver's licence — her grandfather bought her a car before I left for Stroud. She was almost two years older than me. He also bought her a fur coat, which she immediately laid between two mattresses on her bed. "Out of sight," she said to me. "How can I wear a fur coat in Ponty?" I knew what she meant!

The same week, again on my way home from the village, I had just passed the police station, when a young policeman, was out and almost on my heels. He followed a few yards behind me as far as Joyce Thomas' shop and by then I was getting annoyed.

I turned around and I asked him outright "Are you following me?"

He replied "Yes."

I said "Then I hope you have got a good explanation! As I am sure your superior would want one!"

He still followed me up to the gate to our house. His name was Eddie Lewis he told me. *I* was beginning to "take the Mickey" by now; I said, I cannot take that as truth — you could be a relative of "Jack the Ripper" as far as I know!

He started to chuckle, "How about going to the Lyric with me this week, there is a good film on?"

I thanked him and said, "No I won't!"

"How about next week then?" he chided.

"Maybe," I said.

The following week, he was on the way to meet me and we went to the Lyric Cinema. Mary Baggott, the owner's daughter, was in the ticket booth. He talked and talked, I thought of leaving. Eventually he came, and we went downstairs and saw the rest of the film. He saw me home and said "I'll take the 'barley way' back to the police station. I often walk the 'beat' around that way and there are many bats out at night — they fly straight at me; I have to beat them off; they are attracted by the shiny buttons of my uniform!" I was beginning to feel I was the 'batty one'!

34

Mary Baggott told me, he did not want to pay for me to go into the cinema! Policemen have a "free" pass to the cinema but he was annoyed when she told him he had to pay for me. Furthermore, he was disliked by his comrades at the station — he always reckoned he could 'get a date' with any new young lady before the week was out, and once he had collected the bets, he was looking for the next victim!

Back in the office, it seemed both Aussie and I were fairly busy most of the time, as the weeks fled by. Ding was not a shorthand typist, so she dealt with the "copy typing"; which still had to be checked, so it was passed to the other two girls, June and Ollie. Their room always seemed to come alive just before we opened the door. This had been going on for some time and we thought we would catch them out! Quietly the three of us crept out of our room, across the landing and opened their door! There sat both of them, feet up, knitting woollens for the lads "up there"!

June enlightened us by explaining the lads she had been going out with, flew in heavy bombers at night, and inside those bombers it could be freezing cold! Ding looked amazed.

Aussie with eyes widened, said "Is that so?"

And I got a "bright idea"! They were knitting sets of "balaclava helmets", "knee caps" and "mittens" in Air Force blue wool; to keep the lads warm. I was a very good "knitter" and although I would have to change the colour of the wool to khaki, I managed to get them finished in a week. Now I was clever at school in Languages, Maths and Science, hopeless in Geography, but my package was posted immediately and when it reached its destination, Gibraltar, all the lads gathered round Jack, waiting for him to share whatever was to be eaten, something to tickle the taste buds they thought. Of course, when they found out it was mittens, balaclava and knee caps, they all fell around in fits of laughter, and said, "If she's that daft — she might marry you!" Needless to say, they did come in handy — he was able to polish his boots with them!!!

It was sometime since I had seen any of the girls from Holloway Institute, until Miss Clements rang me one day, to see whether I could meet up with them one Saturday morning in Stratford Park. She wanted to take some snaps of her "girls", and I was one from the first group.

A kind gentleman offered to take us as a group. Then one at a time, we were photographed by Miss Clements. When my turn came, I was sitting on the edge of a fairly high wall, banking a large bed of shrubs — when together they chorused "Kathleen don't move!" Normally I would have, but there was panic in the negative *don't*. Then they chorused "It's OK now!"

I said "What was all that about?" Miss Clements and Miss Laughey told me that as I sat there, an enormous long snake was slithering along the ground at the back of me. I think my heart would have stopped had I seen it.

The following week, when I got to my office and settled in to see what order my work should take, an HCO came up to me and asked me whether I knew a girl from Wales whose name he had written on a card.

I said yes, I did know her, although not very well; she worked in clerical and lived up near Stroud Hospital.

He told me, sadly, she was killed that morning, running for the bus as usual. The road was extremely steep from the hospital to the main road, and nearing the bus stop she slipped and went under the bus. He asked me whether I could go around the offices and collect donations to send to her family; which I did; but with a heavy heart.

I was still seeing Charles and we were enjoying each other's company; he was calling regularly at my billet; if he missed coming, they were disappointed, but usually he would be on leave.

Charles was now back from his week's leave and I could hardly wait to see him again; we always had so much to talk about; although strangely, we never exchanged photographs of each other, somehow neither of us thought of it.

We went to the park and he gave me the regular packet of lean turkey, his mother had cut for him; then surprisingly he asked me whether I would like to go to the pub which he and the lads frequented during the evenings each week, except when he was seeing me. It was in Stroud, the bar was long and oval and on one side was Johnny and six or seven of his mates, all enjoying a tankard of ale. He introduced me and suddenly asked me to excuse him a moment, he had to 'pop outside'.

As I stood alone, opposite the lads, Johnny came over and asked me how much did I like Charles.

I said "He is the nicest lad I have met so far."

Johnny said "He is going to ask you to go home to Lincoln on his next leave!"

When we left the pub, he did ask me to go with him to meet his folks; I was already panicking, as I understood he and his girlfriend were expected to marry one day and both 'sets' of parents were looking forward to that day very much. The feeling which nagged at me, was that maybe I would not be welcome, so I said "I don't think so."

The following Monday, he rang me from Lincoln at my office, to say, as he could not come to Mrs Powell's on our next date, could I meet up with him halfway along the main road.

I saw him walking towards me, he said "Kathleen, I have promised Dorothy, I won't see you any more! She has cried most of our leave, and wants to get married on my next leave! I have worried, how I was going to tell you. I hope you won't think bad of me? I have enjoyed all our time together, I can't emphasise how much."

I told him that I had too (although I felt I had been "hit by a brick!"). I hoped they would both be happy.

We parted, he did not look back. I retraced my steps to Mrs Powell's and told her that I would not be seeing Charles any more. We had 'broken up' amicably and I wished him all happiness in his forthcoming marriage.

She said "I'm sorry — we did think something would come of your friendship, you both seemed made for each other."

Then I went to bed early.

She in turn, had heard from George, who told her he had been dating a very nice ATS officer; they liked one another and were getting on well, when her father, a high-ranking army officer, looked into "George's history" and found out he was a Dr Barnardo boy. He had George posted as far away as possible from his daughter! So he was now stationed much further away than usual.

Although I was fine at the office, for the next fortnight — when I came home, I went to my room and suddenly, the tears would flow, until Mrs Powell stepped in and told me that if I did not "pull myself together", she was writing to Mam and Dad, asking them to come and take me home, and she meant it. I did try hard.

Out in the wash house on that particular Friday evening, I took my time preparing to wash my hair first, so I sat on one of the chairs and let my eyes take in the whole scene; it was untidy, although a clean wash house. I looked around, then got quite a shock; up in the corner of the adjoining wall, with no. 4, was a small hole? I hoped it did not show what I thought it might! I managed to reach the height needed, to look through the hole. I could see everything inside no. 4 clearly.

I had been with Mrs Powell for almost two and a half years, and believe Norman Ersell, the elder son, had had more than an eyeful of me, each Friday night!

I was in the mood to knock on his door and blacken both his eyes!

Chapter Four

My Social Life

Back in the office, Ollie said "I'm asking you for the last time, to leave Mrs Powell's and join me at Mrs Smith's. She has a large bedsitting room to let. One guinea per week." She asked me to come up that evening and meet Mrs Smith and see the "room".

Mrs Smith lived at "Pagan Hill", not far from Mrs Powell's. It was a slip road leading off to the left of the main road to Stroud, and eventually, it led to Stratford Park; then into Stroud from a different angle.

I met Mrs Smith, a plump rosy-faced lady, quite friendly, yet I felt she could be determined and aloof if she wanted to. She was more business-like. She showed me the room; it was beautiful and tastefully furnished with the best pieces; also a large four foot six bed. There were to be no visits from men friends. Should I wish to rent it, there were a few rules. It had to be kept tidy and Friday evenings she expected the room to be cleaned and polished throughout. It was nicer than I expected and I decided to move in the next day. Cleaning and polishing were second nature to me, I liked to see a room look tidy.

When I arrived home that evening, I told Mr and Mrs Powell I was going up to Pagan Hill, and renting a fully furnished bedsit, my friend at the office was already renting there.

She asked me what part of Pagan Hill, as she had friends on the lower road; but I was, she said on the 'posher' part. She and Arth were going to miss me, although I told her, I would be calling round to see them from time to time, on my way home possibly, from Ryeford Hall.

Bobby was still stationed on the border of Stonehouse, so Ollie saw quite a lot of him. He was quite tall, about six feet, dark haired, smart, polite with a good sense of humour. If they were going anywhere special, he wore his 'dress uniform' and looked elegant.

June popped in one evening, all boy chat! She said, there was a dance coming up at Aston Down Aerodrome and she suggested we both went. I had no intention of going with June, when Bobby suggested Ollie go as well. He said he did not mind, and Ollie agreed — she said I could then try out my new skills partnered by a man, instead of her!!

I had recently bought myself a nice short-sleeved dress, with a pretty "sweetheart" neckline, but my lack of inches at the top, was obvious! Ollie had the bright idea of padding my bra with cotton wool; and it did look better!

However, we waited in Stroud with a couple of friends and shared a taxi to the 'drome. It worked out 1/- (5p) each. June cancelled out, at the last moment; I think her neighbour's son had arrived home on leave, and was given the use of their classy sports car.

All went well. There was a large buffet and we only drank orange juice. I was fine with the dancing, I had more confidence, and I had several invitations for the "next dance" — when suddenly, I spied a couple of pieces of 'cotton wool'. The more the evening wore on, the more pieces were being kicked around! I had lost about four inches from the top by the time we decided to leave; although it had been great fun. I was beginning to feel less tense.

One strange rule in favour of temporary staff was, that you were allowed six weeks' sick leave per annum, each year. A clerical officer came into the office with a large register and spoke to the temps and said to me, "Have you any idea when you will be likely to take your sick leave?"

I quickly replied "When I'm sick!!"

She was adamant, she was not teasing me, but I was entitled to six weeks per annum.

Then I asked her whether the Air Ministry had a "suggestion box" at all?

"What for?!"

I said, "I have an idea which would be most helpful to me; instead of six weeks' paid sick leave — why not cut out the sick leave, and raise the wages of temps like myself, who are living on the breadline?"

Mary was still writing letters home, but I was not bothered about her any more. I decided instead on my next week's leave, if Mam asked what I was up to, I would embroider stories to fit Mary's skeletal outlines. 1. There was Cyril from Bromley in February. 2. A lad from Brighton was next in March. 3. Then both dumped for a sergeant from Scotland in April! All these lads were supposed to be from local Aston Down Aerodrome. They were mythical, but I was seeing the funny side of Mary, sad in a way — but it made me feel I was playing the lead part in a film!

So, on my next leave, I was ready for cross-examination!

During the evenings, we just sat and chatted. Suddenly, Mam asked if I was still seeing Cyril? I said "Oh him, that was a long time ago."

Sister Enid, jumped up and reached for a calendar hanging under the "mother clock". She said "You were going with Cyril in February, a boy from Brighton in March and a sergeant from Scotland in April!"

These lads were all set out in order, one under the other, and opposite their name, the particular month I was going with them! So if I was "out late at night" and got into trouble, they would know "who did it!!"

After my week's holiday, I was sitting on the bus to Swansea, on the long seat near the door. When we neared Morriston, and the bus stopped, a gentleman around sixty years entered. He sat on the long seat opposite me. He was looking rather serious. Then our eyes met. I smiled at him. He looked puzzled; and our eyes met again, so I smiled again!

Holding on to the rail in the bus, he leaned forward and said "Are you one of my girls?"

I said "Yes I was!"

He continued "Are you Lorraine Lethaby?"

I said "No. Lorraine Lethaby was head prefect when I passed into your school. My name is Kathleen Healy. My sister Mary Healy was also at Ystalyvera."

"Oh, I see" he smiled.

He alighted before I reached Swansea Station, and as he did, he whispered "I'm so glad you're not Lorraine Lethaby!"

His name was Mr Henry Rees our headmaster (IYS) at that time, 1934–1938.

I was receiving more letters from Gibraltar now; and a few snaps besides. Then one day I opened a package — it had two nice bananas. The news shot through the building. No one could get bananas, so I thought the best thing was to raffle them and give the proceeds to charity. One of the girls in clerical who won a banana, sat and ate it *all* herself. We all chorused, "We hope it makes you sick!!"

I had a birthday coming up but I never mentioned it. The particular day arrived and I was first in the office with Ding, as I usually was, when she said "Would you like to come to my bedsit this evening? You know the road where I live. I'll give you the number. Come around 7 p.m., we can have a cosy chat."

I said "I'd love to — see you around 7 p.m. then."

It was behind the boys' college which was on the main Stroud Road, about fifteen minutes' walk away from my bedsit. A lady answered the door and showed me the flat which Ding rented — it was on the ground floor. I buzzed outside the door. Suddenly it opened to the thumping of, "Happy birthday to you, happy birthday to you dear Kathleen . . ."

Ding was at the piano, thumping away. Then when she stopped playing "three well-known" faces popped up from behind her settee! Aussie, Ollie and June! "Thank God for that" said Aussie, "I was beginning to get cramp in my legs." They chorused "And so say all of us."

We had a good 'singsong' and enjoyed cups of steaming cocoa and some toasted crumpets! Another birthday to remember fondly.

The days turned into weeks and I was beginning to accept that I would not see Charles again. I never went into Stroud alone, only Saturdays. It was comfortable at my bedsit. Ollie and I were in and out of each other's rooms, chatting; but on my own at night, I sometimes shed a few tears. I had to pull myself together, as soon I would be sitting an examination for the Civil Service; if I got through, it would be a permanent job, and no doubt I would return with them to London to Adastral House. Then my qualifications would be taken into account and it would be worth my while monetarily, and pensionable. I was not aware, but had I decided to join one of the forces, I would probably have been offered a commission as second lieutenant immediately. I could still have been a shorthand secretary.

The examination was coming up on the Saturday at Holloway Institute. I did not feel worried about it, in fact, I looked forward to it. So I ambled along, giving myself plenty of time. I bought a newspaper, walked past Holloway Institute and made my way down Gloucester Road to the café. I went to the furthest end of the café where there was a small corner, out of sight of the main café. I asked for a cup of tea, and started to read the paper. It did not register. I kept reading the same parts and still did not know what I was reading, then the tears started. I kept as quiet as I could, time crept onwards yet my examination never arose in my mind. I must have sat there two hours, when suddenly, someone lowered my newspaper.

I looked up and saw Charles. He said "You did not turn up for your examination this morning. I came down and wanted to wish you luck. You had not arrived. I went back and they told me they had not seen or heard from you! Please Kathleen, don't get upset, I'm thinking of you too, and I miss you. Can I walk you home?"

I said "I don't live at Mrs Powell's any more. I'll be all right."

We chatted for a while then we parted.

I walked into Cainscross, and thought I'll pop in and see Mr and Mrs Powell. She gave me a hug and said, "Fancy two surprises in the same morning."

George was on his feet too, and was shaking my hand, and giving me one of his teasing smiles. "Nice to see you Kathleen" and he meant it. When I got up to leave, he said "I'll walk you home."

We walked slowly up to Pagan Hill past the Maypole and further on to Mrs Smith's. He stopped and took my hand in his. "Look after yourself

Kathleen and keep well." I thanked him and wished him the same. He walked away and I stood watching until he went out of view; crossed my fingers and whispered, "Please God bring him safely through this war!"

On one occasion, my only ever visit, Mary and I happened to be home at the same time, each not knowing the other was going home. She had met Desmond the previous year, at a small dance held in St Peter's School Room. I remembered we were both there, and this man came and asked me to dance; I had never seen him before. Mary was sitting in the corner, wearing an exceptionally pretty blouse in daffodil coloured silk.

This man asked me whether I knew the girl in the corner.

I told him "Yes, she's my sister."

He said "Could you give me an introduction?"

I did. As normally, she did not dance, wasn't interested, and would always reply "No thank you, I'd rather develop my head than my feet." This together with a 'frozen look'; would be enough to drive them away.

However, this was different, and I walked home alone; and from then on, she would be meeting Desmond and go off on his motorbike. He visited her in Stroud from time to time.

I suppose after six months or so, again, I happened to be home and she was telling Mam, she was going to get married to Desmond fairly soon. Mam flatly refused to listen, she was not going to marry Desmond; not if Mam could help it. So Mary threw herself onto the floor, kicking her heels in temper; by now in a frenzy, when Mam stepped over her and slapped her face hard. She never expected Mam's reaction, but it sobered her up, and she composed herself.

Mam told her, "I know every branch of that family and they are very friendly, yes, but they are all 'work shy'. If you marry him, you will go out to work to keep him."

So it was a quiet wedding at St Peter's Church. Mary, Dad, Desmond and his brother and myself. And they left for their honeymoon as soon as they had eaten, travelling on Desmond's motorbike.

Ollie and I always walked to Ryeford Hall. She also had a bicycle which she kept at work, and used it to see Bobby in the lunch hour. As we left Mrs Smith's, each working day, she ran downstairs and always jumped the last two steps whilst holding on to the head of the post at the bottom. She swung herself round the post. I said "You'll do that once too often and come a cropper!"

Mrs Smith usually had the wireless on loud, and this particular morning, we heard the voice of Sir Winston Churchill. He gave us strength and we both thought, it won't be long; and the war will be over.

Ollie and I, almost read each other's thoughts, I said to her on the way, "Penny for them."

She replied "I've a good mind to go and have my palm read. I've heard of a lady in Stroud, who only charges one shilling (5p) to tell your fortune."

I said "I'm game. Can I come? Although if we don't like what she says, we shall be unhappy!"

My mam always said "Your life is planned out for you 'by the one above'."

She said, "Well let's go, she might tell me something special, which I already know."

I said "Then don't tell me!"

One evening, after work, we rang the bell at this address. A lady asked us into her lounge. She held Ollie's palm first and told her, "You are expecting a baby but you won't carry it; I'm sorry to say." My turn followed. She told me "You are going to meet a man. You have not met him yet; and he will take you all around the world!"

(I was over the moon.) I said "Whoopee!"

With that, her husband came through the front door, and almost threw us out. He was still shouting at his wife as we went down the pathway.

She looked further and said "I can see children in your life, two maybe three, it is not clear, so maybe two."

Ollie miscarried at four months and I met the man she mentioned. It was Jack my pen pal and yes, he has taken me practically around the world! Twenty countries in all, including America!

Back in Ryeford Hall, there was talk that many of us would be returning to Stroud, to the Imperial Hotel, opposite Holloway Institute. Both buildings looked out to the station approach; and Imperial Hotel was now refurbished! Or so they said.

That morning, I sat at my desk, on which there was a large batch of beige postcards — each one, a "prisoner of the Germans". I had to notify the parents, and I was surprised to see the first one, was a lad from Pontardawe!

My dad sometimes called in the British Legion for a beer on his way home from the steelworks, in Ynisderw Road, when he did not go to the working men's club. He had seen the sadness of the parents there, not knowing if their son was killed or a prisoner of war?

Although we kept 'up-to-date' with our work, it could be a further four weeks before they would receive the confirmation, he was safe. I never knew why there should be a delay at all, as our backs and "sit upons", ached from the pressure of typing constantly on typewriters which were only fit enough for the scrapheap!, although we did have the luxury of proper desks, unlike the Holloway Institute where the desks had inkwells!!

Although I had signed "The Secrets Act", I wrote to my father telling him to pass the news to his parents that he was a prisoner of war; but on no account to divulge the source of the information.

Dad wrote "I wish you could have seen their faces, they were crying, then laughing and drinks were free for the week!" Their son's health, and eventual release, was being toasted by all.

Ollie left Ryeford Hall and Mrs Smith's, when Bobby got posted away from Stonehouse. She would eventually live in South Shields, she thought. Bobby's parents and brother and sister were living there.

I moved out of Mrs Smith's almost immediately and got a "registered billet" in Stroud, near the hospital. It was no. 3 Upperfield Terrace, Horns Road. The name was given to me, by one of the new office girls I was to meet at our new Imperial Hotel office. She was clerical and her friend had recently left the billet and also Stroud.

Our little group at Ryeford Hall were 'split up'. Ding (Olive) would have returned to Adastral House, Kingsway. Young June was to return with her parents to Essex and possibly her father would be at Adastral House, and travel by tube to work, from their home in Romford, Essex. Aussie was working in Subscription Rooms, and she also changed her billet from the farm with Miss Sellars. She rented a bedsit on the road above my new billet, so I did see Aussie from time to time in her bedsit. We were all sorry to be breaking up. Miss Clements and Miss Laughey at Holloway Institute had made their way back to London. I never saw them again. Eileen Lloyd had gone home with Leonard. I'm not sure where he was posted to. The only recognised face was Barbara, from the Railway Hotel. When she saw me, she threw herself into my arms, and giggled and giggled. Gone was the nervous, screwed up young girl who had to put up with Eileen's tantrums!! After the episode of the 'inkwell' full of ink, spilling over Eileen's clothes, Eileen no longer called the tune! Myself, I made a point of calling to see Mrs Swales, a couple of Saturday afternoons; and it was so homely. I knitted her a nice pair of woollen gloves with a gift of Yardley talc from Boots the chemist.

My new landlady Mrs Maller, or Hilda as I called her, was early thirties; her husband Bill possibly forty-ish. The family ran a business in Stroud near Woolworth's — plumbing/ironmongery/gardening, quite a flourishing trade. Hilda took no part in the business. Bill's brother and both sons also worked for the family.

Hilda was sprightly, had ginger hair which was plaited and rolled round in a bun at the back of her head. Everything she did was done "at the double", and the love of her life was her cat! Mornings had me rushing downhill all the way to the office, as Hilda gave her cat a "facial" most days! I was asked if I would hold him in a bath towel, while she swabbed his eyes, cleaned his ears, with TCP. He was a handsome ginger tom and the best looked-after cat for streets around; but this regular chore was becoming a strain and I could have killed that cat!!

Hilda visited us regularly each year at Epping, for the last ten years of her life, having lost Bill. We would drive to Stroud and pick her up, and two weeks later, take her home. She looked forward to these breaks.

Imperial Hotel had no atmosphere, it was far too full. Space between desks was just enough to lever yourself out of your seat without stepping on someone's toes or accidentally knocking something off their desks. I saw none of my first friends, apart from Barbara. We were now secretaries and clerical in the same room, possibly twenty of us. We seemed to be the remnants from various departments gathered together in a suffocating atmosphere.

As for this being refurbished; what a nonsense. The stench of gas from the bathrooms, which found its way to us, was not healthy. The girls near the open windows looked out most of the day and we had to get our shorthand typed in a loud noisy atmosphere.

One of the ladies sitting near me, was named Madeline Hellier; possibly in her mid-thirties, very smart and well mannered. What she must have thought of the atmosphere in this room, she kept to herself. She told me, she and her hubby had taken a beautiful country cottage, for renting, opposite the hospital for the duration. It had flowers all around it; very picturesque. Madeline was a shorthand typist, although not permanent staff. She was elegant, her whole appearance was of being well groomed; her long shoulder length hair was blonde, with not a hair 'out of place'. She never wore high-heel shoes, but light strip sandals to match what she wore. She was tall, about five foot seven.

We sometimes met up as we neared the office. Those were the mornings when I had to "hold that cat". Then one evening, we left the office and walked home together and she told me she intended to ask me to dinner sometime; she would let me know. She liked cooking, it occupied the mind, as her husband was serving in the navy; and it was quiet on her own, although she had a nice gramophone and records, it was still quiet.

A short while later, she invited me to dinner at 7 p.m. — I had sufficient time to get to Hilda's and change into my favourite dress. Before I left Hilda's it poured with rain, but I hadn't far to go. Madeline had the dinner started and it smelled beautiful. She said it was a stew with vegetables and dumplings — gorgeous. The cottage inside was as beautiful as outside; the furniture expensive, and comfortable, various chairs covered in bright floral chintz. Rented, fully furnished — it was a boon.

Everything was ready to serve up when the doorbell rang. She answered the door, the laughter and excitement meant it was someone special; she was 'over the moon'; it was her husband! I picked up my handbag and coat and whispered "I'll see you another time."

Her husband, a tall, nice looking naval commander stood there soaked, and with a kind smile said "Oh no you won't! We have enough, plenty, and Madeline cooks a jolly good stew; you must stay. I am pleased to meet you Kathleen. She has told me she had made a friend at the office, a nice young girl named Kathleen."

So I stayed and enjoyed the conversation and the meal, then left early after thanking them for a lovely evening.

It was soon after meeting Hilda and Bill and moving in, I received a letter from Jack. He had left Gibraltar, 3rd May, 1943, and after spending a week with his folk, he was coming to meet up with me in Stroud.

I told Hilda I would be away on two weeks' leave, and hoped to take him to Wales, and I would see her once he had rejoined his company.

Chapter Five

I meet my Pen Friend

I walked the fifteen minutes down to Stroud Station and waited for the train from Paddington to arrive. It was to pull in on the opposite platform. I crossed the bridge, and stood near the steps. The rain had fallen steadily all morning and I did not look my best; but I was excited at meeting my pen friend. The train arrived on time, and with the snapshot of Jack in my hand, I watched the passengers alight; but there was no Jack!

As I turned to leave the platform, an elderly porter near me, said "Don't go away missie, the train is extra long and pulls in twice."

As it slithered to its second halt — with Jack's photo in my hand, the carriage door opened and Jack alighted, holding a snapshot of me in his hand!

We said "Hello". Then I suggested we get back onto the train and travel to its destination which was Swansea, South Wales; to visit my parents. The compartment was almost full of soldiers and we settled in to chat.

By the time we got to Neath Station, Jack was feeling quite tired. He had been travelling from Leyton to Paddington to Stroud and South Wales. Mam was not expecting us, but very pleased to see us. My sister Enid was outside Raglan House, which was the top house on the right-hand side. When she saw us coming up the road, she ran indoors and told Mam, "Our Kath is coming up the road with a soldier, and he can hardly walk!" Both Mam and Dad took to Jack instantly, and we were fascinated by his London accent.

After a meal and a long rest, it was a pleasant evening, so I took Jack for a stroll up to the golf club via the "hundred steps"; this was a short cut through the trees. After half a dozen steps, he was getting short of breath and called out to me, "I'm not going to walk to the top of those steps, so, will you marry me?"

I had been corresponding with Jack for nearly three years and I felt I knew and liked him well. I replied "Yes", and together we walked back to

47

tell Mam and Dad we were getting engaged and married by the end of the year.

They were both happy for us, and said so.

London was getting quite a lot of air raids at this time and Mam wasn't too happy for me to go to London to meet Jack's folks. It was May 1943 and it had been very quiet in Gloucester while I was there. We were having breakfast one morning during Jack's visit. Mam cooked bacon and eggs and laver bread. Jack took one look at the laver bread and said "Oh, I couldn't eat that, no way, it looks like a 'cowpat'!"

Mam said, "If you don't eat it, Kath cannot go to London!" That did it, he held his cup of tea in one hand and a forkful of laver bread in the other; and that way, he washed it down without tasting it; and I went to London!

The Air Ministry were now talking of being settled back in London within a year; so it was planned that I would get married from Jack's home, work at Adastral House and several of my friends would be able to attend.

I spent an enjoyable week in London with Jack. London was vast compared to country and life and even more so from the "top of a London bus!". We stopped at Liverpool Street and Jack bought me a buttonhole of fresh violets. I was quite touched and so excited. People were scurrying in all directions, but a little too fast for me. At the speed they moved, they must have been like robots!

Sitting together one evening, whilst at Jack's home, he said "I think I should write properly to your father and ask him for 'your hand in marriage'."

So that evening he wrote to my father. It was a nice letter. He showed me what he had written, then he popped out and posted it. In his letter to Dad, he stressed that Dad would not be losing a daughter, he would be gaining a son!

Dad's reply, had Jack in stitches. He thanked Jack for his letter, was pleased to welcome him into the family circle, but would he please take the other little so-and-so as well! That was my sister Enid, who was fifteen.

Dad had always teased us about him being the only man with four women in the house! He never got any peace from us, and often threatened; the only way to get some peace, was to build a shed in the garden and live in that!

Chapter Six

In Stroud to accept the Engagement Ring

I returned to Stroud after the fortnight's leave, and moved into my new billet. Hilda, my landlady, was very witty and had a good sense of humour. Her husband Bill, was a kind man, with a smile which spread slowly across his face when I said anything which amused him. We lived in the first house, no. 1, on the end of a row of possibly ten terraced houses. A long path led up from the front entrance to the side of the house and back entrance, which we always used. It was named Upperfield Terrace.

By now, I was earning the vast amount of £2.5.0d. (£2.25p) and I was better off. I still paid £1.1.0d. (£1.05p) for my billet; Hilda asked for no extras, and the food was far superior.

Jack had asked me what design engagement ring I would like, and I said "I would like a half hoop five diamond ring, if not too expensive!" I did not choose one from the jeweller's, they were difficult to get.

Jack's father knew an old Jewish jeweller in Houndsditch, London, who would let him have it at trade price. So with my description, Jack came to Stroud with the 'ring' and we became engaged.

Hilda put him up for the week's leave. She made him a bed up in the attic, and he would go out in the evenings with Bill to the pub on the corner of Horns Road; the road in front of ours, which was a very busy road.

During the daytime, we were out and about, taking in all the scenery, and would call in one of the many pubs for a "drink and a snack". Hilda liked to go to the cinema when there was a good film showing, like "Girl of the Golden West", and at these times, she would meet me coming out of the Imperial Hotel, and wend our way to either the 'Gaumont' or the 'Ritz'. She would hand me a packet of sandwiches she had made for me, and we would sit there 'munching' as we watched — if it was a "weepy", then we munched while the tears dropped!

Although my leisure hours were spent in and around Stroud, I never saw Charles ever again. He didn't seem to come into town as he used to. I

49

did wonder whether he had been posted or not.

Sundays were lovely days for me. The town was quiet, practically empty, and I would sit at home and browse through the Sunday papers. Hilda and Bill always took the papers up to bed after lunch on Sundays, and I remember sitting on my own one Sunday, and after about two hours, thinking I would make them a 'cup of tea' and take it up to them! I must say, they looked pleasantly surprised. I thought later, they probably could have throttled me! My stay at Hilda's was most pleasant.

Stomach pains had been a problem of mine from time to time for the most part of my stay in Stroud, and I must have sucked thousands of "Rennies" during that period.

Jack and I had arranged to get married the week before Christmas, and he was now due for some more leave. This was September, and we met up and travelled on to Wales, for the seven days. It was our second day and we decided to go to Swansea Sands. The stomach pain played overtime, so Jack suggested that I call in the doctor's that morning, for something to relieve the pain.

The doctor examined me and asked me all sorts of questions, such as the length of time I had been experiencing this trouble, and at the same time he continued to scribble on a pad. Eventually, after he had finished writing, he said, "If you are going anywhere near the hospital in Swansea, pop this letter in."

Well, we were going that way to the Sands, so we called into the hospital first. After they had read the letter, I was shown to a cubicle and Jack was asked to wait in the 'waiting room'! A doctor came and examined me and I was told to sit there until someone arrived with a wheelchair and took me to a ward. I was being admitted with suspicions of a "duodenal ulcer" due to malnutrition.

Jack was as surprised as I was. Here he was starting a 'seven-day leave' and he was going to spend it visiting me in hospital. This of course he did, then returned to his unit in Yorkshire.

50

Chapter Seven

Events leading up to my Wedding Day

I was kept in hospital for a month on a strict milk and egg diet (Hurst diet) then I was transferred to the Workingmen's Rest Home in Oystermouth, on the Gower Coast. This building had been taken over by Swansea Hospital as an annexe, and I was to spend almost a further three months there! The ward I was in, faced the sea, and included a further five patients. I did nothing but rest and drink milk with the occasional egg whipped into it. It was an exciting day, if a ship went by!

The other patients in the ward were recuperating or terminal. One very young girl had her index finger removed. She had been washing-up lunch dishes one day, and was about to wash the enamel colander. It had some dry vegetables stuck to it, so she scratched it off with her "fingernail", and a small piece of enamel entered her finger, and the next thing the finger had to be removed. So easily done.

The lady in the bed opposite me, was 'terminal'. She had cancer of the stomach and was only in her thirties. She was very ill. Most of the time, the "screens" were around her bed. Her husband and two small children (a boy and a girl) visited freely. The nursing staff would change her dressings several times a day, during which time, we were advised to snuggle down under the bedclothes, but the odour still permeated through. She was a very pretty lady; we all liked her. She chatted from time to time and knew I was going to get married 18th December coming. She asked me if I would let her have my wedding bouquet? And I did, my father travelled back to Swansea from Leyton, then Paddington, the day after our wedding, with the bouquet, and on reaching Swansea, took the train to Oystermouth to give her the flowers.

The hospital sister at Swansea Hospital, told my father I was to stay for some months. So Dad then went to Stroud to "pick up" my belongings from Hilda's. Billets were very hard to find and I had to give it up; as the Air Ministry needed it. Even so, Hilda and Bill asked my father to stay for a week's holiday and he had a most enjoyable stay with them, and evenings with Bill around the corner at the local pub!

Jack visited me once while I was at Oystermouth. He travelled through the night and had to return by the next evening. It was difficult to reach the rest home.

Mam would get the bus from "Ponty" to Swansea, then a train to Mumbles, alighting at Oystermouth, where, if you were lucky, after a long walk uphill "fortunate" if a bus was waiting at the top to take you to the rest home. More often than not, it would have left, and she would arrive, completely 'out of breath' and exhausted. I begged her not to come all that way, but it was so nice to see her when she did manage to come.

I was still in the hospital annexe and the date was fast approaching for my wedding to Jack. I was anxious to get discharged.

The 'special' day arrived three days before I got married. A nurse came up to my bed, carrying a plate with two fingers of toast and some hot milk, and announced "You can go home today! although you have got to stay on a diet for sometime."

I took a quick 'peep' at my chart — it had "duodenal ulcer" due to malnutrition. This accounted for me being so thin. I was now under eight stones in weight. Mam and Dad were contacted. Mam was still affected by the eczema on her arms, and wasn't too well. Constant irritation from wearing sleeves to her dresses or the weight of her outdoor coat when she came to visit me, was stressful for her, but she came and took me home. I was to report to my own doctor once discharged.

On the Friday, Dad and I travelled to London for my wedding on the following day. Mam did not come, she stayed at home with young sister Enid. Had I known how things were to turn out, and that I was to spend almost four months in hospital, I would have changed plans and married in Wales.

My eldest sister Mary, now lived up in Derby. She worked as a secretary for Rolls-Royce, and had married the summer previously. She was down with rheumatic fever, and could not get to my wedding either. So the only 'friend' we had at the wedding, was dear old "Aussie", a friend of Jack's earlier and of course, she was "special" to both of us. All the other guests, besides Dad, were relatives and friends of Jack's mum and dad; and strangers to me. This was a most unusual wedding, where the bride was the "stranger"!

I wore my Prince of Wales check costume with a large brimmed velour brown hat and shoes to match. My wedding bouquet was beautiful and was given to the lady I got to know whilst in the hospital annexe. She received it the following day when Dad took it to her.

52

We were married in St Edward's Church, Morley Road, Leyton, on Saturday, 18th December, 1943, by "special licence" — issued by the Archbishop of Canterbury's office — Jack was a bombardier at that time. Once pronounced 'man and wife', Jack kissed me, then turned smartly and walked down the aisle! His aunt Nell, in the front pew, grabbed his arm and said "You've got a wife now, you know," and was his face red!

We left later that day by taxi, for the train to Liverpool Street Station, where we continued on to Ely, travelling first-class to Kings Lynn. The train stopped for fifteen minutes at Ely. One of the occupants of the carriage was a rear admiral, a very pleasant gentleman. He alighted when it stopped and returned with some refreshment on a tray, for us.

Arriving in Kings Lynn late that Saturday night, we found it bitterly cold and sleeting, and poor Uncle Ernest waiting for our train to stop. He rushed us into a nearby pub and bought us a drink, then got a taxi home to meet the family and a welcome hot meal waiting for us.

It was especially nice to meet the family, which included Jack's grandmother. She was in her late seventies, and made all her own gowns, still in Edwardian style; a fitted bodice with covered buttons down the centre, high collared and long sleeved. Mornings, she was awake early and took one hour to dress her hair, plaited and worn in a bun at the nape of her neck. She often caught the local bus near the house, when she went visiting. A very capable lady.

Our first morning, Uncle Ernest tapped on the bedroom door and handed us a tray of tea, but before leaving the room, went to the 'bay' window and opened it wide. It was snowing heavily and freezing cold. I jumped up and closed the window, but not before he popped his head around the door, and said "I knew you would do that!"

Uncle Ernest had experienced TB when he was younger and still remembered all the 'fresh air' they were offered as part of their recovery. The bad weather did not deter us from getting around sightseeing. Most of Jack's relatives lived in Kings Lynn, so there were quite a few relatives to visit.

Aunt Ada told me, when she and Uncle Ernest were courting, Jack's mother (sister) was courting Jack's father. The four of them were out together one day, and after some sightseeing, they found a restaurant, and went inside for tea. There wasn't a table for four, but there were two tables for two, one each side of the room, so the two men sat at the table shown to them and the girls sat at the second table. They chose the most expensive cakes, and more than one each. When the assistant handed them the 'bill' — they pointed to the two men, and said, "Those gentlemen will pay the bill!" However, when the men were handed the 'bill' they told the waitress, "The two ladies are not with us. We don't know who they are." So only paying their own 'bill', they left the restaurant! The two girls were asked

53

again to pay their 'bill', and ended up in the 'ladies' room' tipping out the contents of their handbags and coming up with just the amount in small change, to cover the cost of their greed, plus ½d. They were both annoyed and more so when leaving the restaurant to find the two men in stitches with laughter outside, but they came around eventually and knew they had been greedy!

Our second week, we returned to Jack's home for the few days left of his leave, and went out daily by tube, sightseeing, around London.

It was at Lyons Corner House, Leicester Square — we stopped for morning tea and cakes, and listened to the band playing the latest music on the dais. One of the young waitresses, known as "nippies", in her pretty laced edged short pinafore and lace edged cap, with notepad in hand, asked us what we would like. She returned with a tray, pot of tea for two, cups and saucers and two cakes. I poured both cups of tea; Jack was about to pick up his cup and have a drink, but the handle came off in his hand and scalding tea soaked him where it hurt most! She was very embarrassed, trying to dry the lap of his uniform with a towel, but he laughed and told her he was OK.

The following day, he returned to his unit in Yorkshire, near Thorne (Doncaster), and his parents saw me safely onto the Paddington train for Swansea. I arrived home to live with Mam and Dad and wait for the war to end and Jack's demobilisation . . . .

Chapter Eight

The Invasion and After

That wasn't to be for another three years however, so I found a position as a secretary/shorthand typist in the head office of the Mond Nickel Company, whose offices were based for the duration of hostilities at Clydach, just three miles down the valley from Pontardawe. This position I kept until Jack was demobbed. I travelled the three miles by bus, but was allowed sufficient time to get home and back for lunch; they being aware I had to keep to a diet. They were extremely considerate to work for and I appreciated their kindness. Mam kept me to the diet and I recovered and regained the lost weight in a year. I now felt fine.

Jack came home a couple of times on leave from his base at Thorne, Yorkshire, and then went out on the invasion D-day plus 1 — that was six months after we got married. General Eisenhower had sent a message on a leaflet to all troops who were to take part in the invasion, and Jack wrote a letter to me on the reverse side, popped it into an envelope and tossed it out of the carriage window as the train moved out of the station. Some kind person picked it up and posted it for him. I received it safely.

It was quiet living at Pontardawe again, after my absence of three and a half years in Stroud; there was nothing to do. I was quite happy that I was living with Mam and Dad and most evenings we sat and talked. I knitted or started getting things together for the home.

No amount of coaxing would make Mam take more than twenty-five shillings a week for my keep. She advised me to save as much as I could, including my married allowance from Jack who was now a staff sergeant. "You will need all you can save," and of course, as usual, she was right.

Mam had stopped keeping pigs some years earlier and she gave all her chickens away to a man on the Coedcae, named "Gomer Harris", who had lost his job at the local works when they found he was epileptic. She told him, if he liked to bring a "big sack" along to the chicken shed, he could have our hens, so as to start him off on his own. She was always so very generous.

We kept hens only for the eggs. We could never kill a bird and eat it. If Dad suggested killing, or as he normally used the words "ring her neck" and have her for Sunday lunch, the opposition from four females, was so strong, he ended up wishing he had never suggested it.

Dad loved boiled eggs, and when he decided he would make his tea time or breakfast time boiled eggs, three would be normal. He would "cut off" or "tap around", remove the cap, then insert a large lump of butter into each egg! This gave him more yolk, and the yolks he loved.

As a young lad in Ireland, they kept a kettle for boiling eggs. They filled the kettle and the family had as many as they fancied.

Jack was recommended on two occasions for a commission, but he turned it down. He maintained he could send me more money if he did not have "mess bills" to fork out for. So he stayed a staff sergeant/trade.

On the 16th April, 1945, Jack was helping to dismantle "German flash simulators" which were attached to trees in a wood about five miles from Solingen, when, one of them exploded in his face and badly burnt his face and both eyes. He was flown to a hospital in Brussels where he was treated with penicillin, and it was some weeks before he could see, or make out the outline of a nurse walking through the ward. The War Office report was held back by order of Jack. He needed to know if he had "lost his sight" before I was to be informed. However, he was very lucky. He came home on sick leave after being discharged from hospital in Brussels, still minus eyebrows and eyelashes. I received the War Office report later in May 1945.

It was interesting to learn, he had met our neighbours' son, Captain Randall Lewis, who lived opposite us on the Coedcae. Having had a front tooth removed by a military doctor, due to an abscess, he needed a dental plate for the one tooth as he was due for some leave and embarrassed to arrive home with a huge space in the front of his top teeth. Captain Randall Lewis was the dentist who made the plate for Jack. During conversation, Jack told him he was married to a girl from the Swansea Valley. Randall said "Oh! What part?" And when Jack said Pontardawe, he replied, "But I come from Pontardawe. What part of Ponty?" Jack said the Coedcae, her name was Kathleen Healy. "Well, well, what a small world, I know Kathleen and her family well!"

However, Jack was now very pleased to have the false plate so soon, and left to travel through Germany in cattle trucks. It was a very long journey and the trucks were full of soldiers. They were tired and many had decided to lay down and get some sleep. Jack decided he would remove the false plate, and for safety, carefully put it in the top pocket of his battledress. It would have been safe there, had not some "fool" soldier, deciding to walk past, trodden on him and broken it! So he arrived home with a "gap" in his front teeth after all!

Jack was a Territorial soldier, who enlisted at Whipps Cross, Leyton, Essex, on the 22nd February, 1939, for four years. On 24th August, some days prior to the war breaking out, he was mobilised as he was a "key man" in an anti-aircraft battery, he moved to Canvey Island. Subsequently, because of the inactivity, he volunteered to join the Finnish army, because that tiny country had been attacked by the Russians. Eventually, he ended up, two hundred and fifty miles inside the Arctic Circle in Northern Norway, being eventually evacuated to Scotland.

Returning from Norway, 11th June, 1940, he was five days in England, before he left for Gibraltar. Once in Gibraltar, the soldiers found they were to work rock tunnelling, eight hours on shift/eight hours off shift — no mask protection; to build the hospital inside the rock and also to make a runway for planes to take off and land. He wrote a book — the title *"Life on the Rock"* by Bombardier J. Durrant, but he did not publish it. After three and a half years on Gibraltar, he went on the invasion second day of D-day, seeing service in France, Belgium and Germany; six years in all.

I had kept in touch with Hilda and dear "Aussie", and told them Jack was in a Brussels hospital with facial injuries, unable at that time to see, but was being treated with penicillin, which was in its infancy at the time.

Shortly after, I received a letter from Charles, he having met Aussie in Stroud whilst with his wife Dorothy, and Aussie had given him my latest news. He wrote me a very kind letter, hoping Jack would recover completely and we would have a very happy marriage. His PS at the bottom of his letter said — "I thought more of you than you will ever know."

I was quite settled in my work in the head office of the Mond Nickel Company, and became a friend of a local girl sitting opposite me; her name was Nina Facey and we became great friends. Her husband was serving in the Royal Navy. She lived with her parents, in a road behind the Catholic church. She had a nickname for me, she called me "sausage", and the first time she used it was as I was boarding the valley bus for lunch at home. She had been shopping in Swansea, whilst on leave, and previously mentioned "If I see any fresh fish, I will get you some," and sure enough the conductor of my bus waited whilst I dashed to the bus behind to take the package from Nina!

My mother was most excited one lunch hour, when I got home, she showed me quite a heavy parcel, which had arrived that morning from Jack. Quickly I opened one end and saw the most beautiful silk brocade in rose pink and the other in a lovely shade of blue. A whole roll of each!

That evening Mam and I looked at it. I said "What on earth can I use it for?"

Mam said, "I've got an idea. We have a few 'real wool blankets' which are getting rather thin. I suggest they could be laid on top of each other, maybe two or three and stitched together as a heavier blanket. Then covered in the brocade, blue one side, pink the other. They would be perfect as quilts for the bed, and nice and warm besides."

Mam worked for hours, cross-stitching the whole quilt, and made some cushions as well. There must have been more than twenty yards in each roll. She made me two quilts and I gave Mam the remainder, and she was so delighted.

When next we saw Jack, he told us the story regarding the brocade. That was May 1945. They had fought their way through Holland where the people had been so kind to our troops, they had very little to give, but were prepared to share with the lads. When the soldiers had advanced about sixty miles up into Germany, they came across a disused factory which was producing the silk brocade, and was a luxury at that time. All the labour was "slave labour", so Jack and his men got a scammel lorry with towing gear and drove up to the steel doors of the factory. They tore off the doors and inside were hundreds and hundreds of bales of different coloured silk brocade. They packed their lorry full, then drove back to the border village near Venlo, where Jack and his mates knocked on each door, and presented each occupant with two rolls of brocade. These people had been ruthlessly treated by the Germans and had got nothing. He said the look of amazement, then sheer delight was overwhelming.

Chapter Nine

Our First Home

His mother wrote and asked whether she and his father, could come down for a couple of weeks, a break from the continual bombing? This was in September 1944. Of course, we made them welcome. Mam and Dad took them to the Gower and other places of interest.

About the same time, Mary and Desmond had returned from Derby to live close by. They managed to rent two rooms with a young woman advertising 'rooms to let', and on this particular day she was with us lunch time at home. I was about to leave for the office when Jack's mother said "Give me your cup and I'll read it for you!" She told me I was going to hear soon the death of a dark-haired young man. Mam and Enid had no connection, but she saw this young man also, in Mary's cup, so it had to be someone from Stroud.

I looked at Mary, I said "Oh God no, not George." He was the only one we both knew who had dark hair, dark moustache, and he was someone special to me.

Jack's mother told us we would hear the news soon.

I did, about a week later. Hilda sent me a "cutting" from *"The Stroud News & Journal"*. It was a photograph of George in uniform and it told how he was 'killed in action' 6th August, 1944 in Europe. She wrote at the bottom, "I believe this is the young man you spoke so much about."

I was in tears, I could not believe it was true and I know Mr and Mrs Powell would have been devastated; both in their eighties; he was a dear son to them, and Dorothy's loveable brother always.

Jack and I returned to Stroud in 1980. Hilda loaned us her cottage whilst she holidayed at Weston, so we had plenty of time to visit the memorable places I had often relived in my mind.

The first Sunday, we walked from Stroud to Cainscross church, where George had been a member of the church choir, and asked where the War

Memorial was, as the place I remembered it had been, there was no sign of it.

In its place was a parking space for cars; for three extra cars, the Memorial had to go!

A lady walking her dog, told us she was doing just that, and was not far from the Memorial, when suddenly it was blown to pieces. She almost had a heart attack.

Jack wrote to the newspaper, and said the village of Cainscross was aptly named, the mark of Cain had surely done its deed that day. He received many letters from the villagers; they had all opposed the destruction of the Memorial, but someone must have given permission for the deed to be carried out.

Jack's second leave, 17th May, 1945, we spent in London at his parents' home and took in some of the shows running that week. "The Crazy Gang" at the London Palladium, was hilarious. Before the start of the show, they were down among the audience, throwing things at random, most of which were returnable — attached to long elastic strings! The week seemed to fly by, then back to Wales.

Before Jack came home on 'demob leave' December 1945, his father had written to him to ask whether he wished to buy the house they were living in at Leyton, as it had been offered to "sitting tenants" at the low remarkable price of £450. The houses were terraced, bay windowed, three bedroomed and similar rows to this had been demolished by the continuing bombing.

Jack's friends, two brothers — serving overseas, lost all their family — mother, father and sisters, and only one brother was allowed leave to go home and sort out affairs. His parents did not wish to buy it; they had lived in it thirty years. Jack was born in the house. They planned to retire to Kings Lynn where they originally came from. The "offer" being to occupants only, it was to be in their name, until such time as it would be transferred to us as a "deed of gift". Neither of his two brothers were interested in buying it, so we put down a deposit of £145. It was understood we would get possession once his father had retired from the Midland Bank, in the City. In the meantime we put our name down on a housing list in Kent.

Chapter Ten

Our Family

Once Jack was out on demob leave, beginning of January 1946, I travelled up to London to stay with his parents at their home. We lived with them and in May I discovered I was going to have our first child. It was difficult to find a hospital who could place me on their list, and I was not accustomed to the whereabouts of travelling on different number buses to various hospitals. So Jack wrote to the matron at The City of London Maternity Hospital telling her he was a soldier, now demobbed; we were expecting our first child and were unable to get booked in, and as I was a stranger to the area, he was concerned for me.

She immediately wrote and gave me a definite appointment to see her.

I arrived at the hospital and joined about twenty other "mothers-to-be" who were already sitting in rows on wooden forms, waiting for the matron to arrive. Everyone seemed to be looking around hoping to see a well-known face! The young woman directly in front of me, turned around, and I was most surprised to see it was Eileen Lloyd, who originally worked in Holloway Institute! More than four years before.

We were to be 'booked in', examined, then told to use our local clinic up until three weeks before the birth. Then we would have to return to "The City of London Hospital", and there join the bus (nicknamed, the "bump special") which was to take us to "Brocket Hall", the home of Lord Brocket — taken over by City of London Hospital for the duration of hostilities. This was near Welwyn, Hertfordshire.

As I did not see Eileen, I enquired whether she may have already given birth, but I was told, she lost her baby. When the telegram she received from her family, told her that both her father and her sister's husband were killed in the same colliery accident, Eileen had a miscarriage.

Our first son, named Jack Dennis, was born 5th November, 1946, on a cold drizzly day, at 12 a.m., and that thick foggy night, we were told not to expect visitors; it was impossible to see anything!

However, I did have visitors — Jack's brother Len, drove to the hospital with Jack. When they were taken to the nursery, the nurse looked at Jack, she said "Name please?" He replied "Durrant." She took him to see the baby, Len followed. She repeated, "Name please?" Len said "Durrant!" She glared at the two of them, then said "What are you — joint fathers!?"

My family visited us regularly while we lived in Leyton, if not together, then separately; and Enid's fiancé William, called regularly, when he was transferred to the head office of the Mond Nickel Company, based in London.

Strangely, the doorbell rang around 7 p.m. and the TV series was "Just William"!

It was later when they married and came to us for their honeymoon, we decided to play a trick on them; actually on Enid. Once seated for the meal, Jack popped outside the back garden, and picked up our pet rabbit, and put him on the floor. We resumed our meal, when suddenly Enid's face looked shocked. She remarked, as the rabbit moved about, "Oh! Hasn't that cat got long ears!!" But we got our comeuppance for playing that trick, as the rabbit bit into the TV lead, all went dead, except the rabbit. He still hopped about, of course it was a laugh, so funny!

The Bakers Arms at Leyton was our nearest shopping centre, then Walthamstow market, a little further on, that was a "shopper's" dream. Jack had warned me about the "wide boys" who sold from their suitcases, shouting "I ain't here today and gone tomorra!" I could not believe my ears. He was selling ladies' best silk stockings for a fraction of the normal price, in fact a 'give-away' price. Of course I fell for it. I said I'll have two pairs please. He wrapped up the stockings, cut out my coupons (from the book) and I gave him the money. I got home, told Jack. He said, "No not you. I warned you. Let me see them."

Out of the two pairs, there wasn't one stocking the same length! We had to laugh, one stocking was at least a foot longer than the others, the second, the toes were not stitched; there was something wrong with them all. He would have made a nice profit, as it was the 'coupons' which he wanted; he could sell those and make a handsome profit.

The fruit and veg was the best bargain on the stalls, if you left your shopping to around 3 p.m. on a Saturday!

Another time, Mam and I were browsing at the Bakers Arms, and were about to catch the next trolley bus home. At that particular bus stop, there were several shops, a cinema, and a large open front display of wet fish at the last shop. As the trolley bus slid silently to our stop, just as we were about to board it, Mam said to the conductor, "Hang on a minute please, I want to buy a pair of kippers!"

He looked at her and said "Lady! You're either on or you're off!"

So Mam looking disappointed, boarded the bus.

Our second son Michael was born nearer home, at Queen Mary's Hospital in Stratford, East London, late evening 19th December, 1950. He was named after my uncle Michael who was killed in the 1914–18 War; a much decorated soldier, aged twenty-five years, having won the DCM, MM and BAR, an the Albert Medal.

We moved from Leyton after eight years and bought a new house in 1954 in Epping, Essex; where we lived for thirty-two years. Both boys grew into fine men and both graduated with 2:1 Honours Degrees.

I am now seventy-seven years of age and my husband eighty-one years of age, and retired to Langtoft, Lincolnshire in 1986.

The Meeting — Stroud Station 1943

The station where we met way back in 1943
Has never changed, is still the same, for anyone to see;
I remember waiting for your train to stop at platform one,
The rain fell down in torrents, when it stopped you hadn't come.
I thought you'd let me down, so I slowly climbed the stairs,
"Hang on young Miss — this train stops twice," said the porter in my ear.
I slowly turned, came down the stairs and stood on platform one,
With a picture of a soldier in my hand.
The train it stopped, and there you were, about to leave the train,
And you looked the smartest soldier in the land.
We both climbed back onto the train and travelled on to Wales
To meet my folk and get to know me better.
We fell in love, made plans to wed, and the rest is plain to see,
That we owe it all, to writing all those letters.

Wartime Memories

Away from home at sixteen
The war was on and I was keen
To do my bit as best I could,
So off I went to Gloucester's STROUD,
To billet in a cottage small
Near water's edge and that's not all;
The folk were friends in every way
And made me welcome there to stay,
And in a building oh, so big
I'd type away from 9 till 6 —
With break for lunch, if you could call,
A tiny snack or sausage roll.
Four years it was, and I grew up
And found that life could be abrupt;
I'd type for hours and feel despair,
For all the lads we lost up there.
To tell loved ones the news was sad,
Gripped me inside and made me sad.

And when the work each week was done,
We'd ride uphill to ASTON DOWN,
To join the boys and there perchance,
To stay awhile and sing and dance.
But other times, we'd look around
At all the Cotswold beauty found;
The Fort at Rodborough, The Common,
And further on there's Minchinhampton;
And now for breath, just wait a tick —
Never shall I forget dear PAINSWICK!
Birdlip, Bisley, Sheepscombe, Stonehouse,
A paradise of wealth about us.
Now years have passed — sixty in all
And I went back on them to call,
To reminisce and see once more
This beauty I knew long ago.

Country Wealth

Beauty in the hedgerows and in the fields I find
Can outweigh the chosen blooms of any other kind;
They may be few and far between and difficult to see,
But if you come across them, you'll understand the need —
To let them flourish as they are, not plunder or disturb,
Because there's very few of them, some of them unheard.
Some hide behind much bigger growth,
Others stand out proud.
Please cherish them, not covert them,
Let them survive the crowd.

Reflections

He sits on the green at the end of the town
Gazing at the moving scene with time to spare,
No doubt reliving years gone by
When life was simpler and pollution never filled the air.

What thoughts I wonder, filter through his mind,
Maybe when he was a boy and life went on
At a much slower pace than that today?
Memories so fresh in mind of times now gone.

A well-worn face with laughter lines laid deep
And sorrow too, sometimes his eyes do show.
What thoughts has he of present life today?
I'd like to stop awhile and maybe get to know.

He must be eighty if he is a day.
Perhaps he thinks of loved ones now no more,
Or maybe coping with the present stress of life
And finds our endless rush and tear, a needless bore?

Nature's Treasure

Have you walked into the forest
And seen the beauty there?
Not only in the trees themselves
But small growth everywhere.
Around some trees the fungi grow,
The colours are supreme;
There's yellow, orange, beige and brown,
These really must be seen;
They cling around the barks of trees,
Some pop up through the ground.
Be careful where you tread the earth,
They're waiting to be found;
Though not to be disturbed or cut,
For they are Nature's treasure.
It's nice to think you've seen them too,
Let others share the pleasure.